EFFECT OF THE
HIPAA PRIVACY RULE
ON HEALTH RESEARCH

Proceedings of a Workshop Presented to the National Cancer Policy Forum

National Cancer Policy Forum

Roger Herdman and Harold Moses, *Rapporteurs*

INSTITUTE OF MEDICINE
OF THE NATIONAL ACADEMIES

THE NATIONAL ACADEMIES PRESS
Washington, D.C.
www.nap.edu

THE NATIONAL ACADEMIES PRESS   500 Fifth Street, N.W.   Washington, DC 20001

NOTICE: The project that is the subject of this report was approved by the Governing Board of the National Research Council, whose members are drawn from the councils of the National Academy of Sciences, the National Academy of Engineering, and the Institute of Medicine.

This study was supported by Contracts No. HHSN261200611002C, 200-2005-13434, TO #1, HHSM-500-2005-00179P, HHSP23320042509XI, TO #4, 223-01-2460, TO #27, HHSH25056133, TO #6 between the National Academy of Sciences and, respectively, the National Cancer Institute, the Centers for Disease Control and Prevention, the Centers for Medicare and Medicaid Services, the Agency for Healthcare Research and Quality, the Food and Drug Administration, and the Health Resources and Services Administration. Support was also received from the American Cancer Society, the American Society of Clinical Oncology, C-Change, and UnitedHealth Group. Any opinions, findings, conclusions, or recommendations expressed in this publication are those of the author(s) and do not necessarily reflect the view of the organizations or agencies that provided support for this project.

International Standard Book Number 0-309-10291-X

Additional copies of this report are available from the National Academies Press, 500 Fifth Street, N.W., Lockbox 285, Washington, DC 20055; (800) 624-6242 or (202) 334-3313 (in the Washington metropolitan area); Internet, http://www.nap.edu.

For more information about the Institute of Medicine, visit the IOM home page at: **www.iom.edu**.

Printed in the United States of America.

The serpent has been a symbol of long life, healing, and knowledge among almost all cultures and religions since the beginning of recorded history. The serpent adopted as a logotype by the Institute of Medicine is a relief carving from ancient Greece, now held by the Staatliche Museen in Berlin.

"Knowing is not enough; we must apply.
Willing is not enough; we must do."

—Goethe

INSTITUTE OF MEDICINE
OF THE NATIONAL ACADEMIES

Advising the Nation. Improving Health.

THE NATIONAL ACADEMIES
Advisers to the Nation on Science, Engineering, and Medicine

The **National Academy of Sciences** is a private, nonprofit, self-perpetuating society of distinguished scholars engaged in scientific and engineering research, dedicated to the furtherance of science and technology and to their use for the general welfare. Upon the authority of the charter granted to it by the Congress in 1863, the Academy has a mandate that requires it to advise the federal government on scientific and technical matters. Dr. Ralph J. Cicerone is president of the National Academy of Sciences.

The **National Academy of Engineering** was established in 1964, under the charter of the National Academy of Sciences, as a parallel organization of outstanding engineers. It is autonomous in its administration and in the selection of its members, sharing with the National Academy of Sciences the responsibility for advising the federal government. The National Academy of Engineering also sponsors engineering programs aimed at meeting national needs, encourages education and research, and recognizes the superior achievements of engineers. Dr. Wm. A. Wulf is president of the National Academy of Engineering.

The **Institute of Medicine** was established in 1970 by the National Academy of Sciences to secure the services of eminent members of appropriate professions in the examination of policy matters pertaining to the health of the public. The Institute acts under the responsibility given to the National Academy of Sciences by its congressional charter to be an adviser to the federal government and, upon its own initiative, to identify issues of medical care, research, and education. Dr. Harvey V. Fineberg is president of the Institute of Medicine.

The **National Research Council** was organized by the National Academy of Sciences in 1916 to associate the broad community of science and technology with the Academy's purposes of furthering knowledge and advising the federal government. Functioning in accordance with general policies determined by the Academy, the Council has become the principal operating agency of both the National Academy of Sciences and the National Academy of Engineering in providing services to the government, the public, and the scientific and engineering communities. The Council is administered jointly by both Academies and the Institute of Medicine. Dr. Ralph J. Cicerone and Dr. Wm. A. Wulf are chair and vice chair, respectively, of the National Research Council.

www.national-academies.org

NATIONAL CANCER POLICY FORUM

ELLEN STOVALL, President and CEO, National Coalition for Cancer Survivorship

JANET WOODCOCK, Deputy Commissioner for Operations, Food and Drug Administration

Staff

SHARYL NASS, Senior Program Officer
ROGER HERDMAN, Director, National Cancer Policy Forum
ALIZA NORWOOD, Research Assistant
MARY ANN PRYOR, Senior Program Assistant

Contents

1

Introduction

The President's Cancer Panel's (the Panel) 2003 Annual Report, *Living Beyond Cancer: Finding a New Balance* made a number of recommendations on issues affecting cancer survivors across the life span. Among them, under the heading of HIPAA Privacy and Insurance Portability Provisions (see Box 1), were recommendation 3a, "The Institute of Medicine should be commissioned to evaluate the impact of HIPAA provisions and provide guidance to legislators on amendments needed to make this law serve the interests of cancer survivors and others" and 3b, "HIPAA privacy provisions (called the Privacy Rule) inhibiting the ability to track and collect data for research on cancer survivors should be re-evaluated" (Reuben, SH, Ed., 2004). The Panel's 2005–2006 report, *Assessing Progress, Advancing Change*, called again for an evaluation of HIPAA-related barriers (Reuben, SH, Ed., 2006).

Panel member Margaret L. Kripke, PhD, Executive Vice President and Chief Academic Officer, the University of Texas M. D. Anderson Cancer Center, requested time to address the Institute of Medicine's (IOM) National Cancer Policy Forum (the Forum) at its February 22, 2006 meeting. At that meeting, Dr. Kripke presented herself as a messenger from the President's Cancer Panel regarding the Panel's findings and recommendations on the impact of HIPAA on research. She referred to the Panel's 2003 report in which the Panel found that the HIPAA Privacy Rule slowed research on cancer survivors. She also mentioned increased bureaucracy, informed consent problems, and complications for clinical trials as ways in which the

Box 1

History of the Privacy Rule: The Health Insurance Portability and Accountability Act (HIPAA) of 1996 (Public Law 104-191) was enacted to improve the portability and continuity of health insurance; combat waste, fraud, and abuse in health insurance and health care delivery; promote medical savings accounts; improve access to long-term care services and coverage; and *simplify the administration of health insurance*. The Administrative Simplification "Standards for Privacy of Individually Identifiable Health Information" (the Privacy Rule) arise from this last objective. HIPAA's Administrative Simplification provisions focus on facilitating the electronic exchange of information for financial and administrative functions related to patient care. However, the very advances that make it easier to transmit information also present challenges to preserving the confidentiality of potentially sensitive personal information contained in medical records. Absent further congressional action, the Secretary of Health and Human Services (HHS) was required by the law to develop standards for protecting such information. Within HHS, the Office for Civil Rights (OCR) is responsible for implementing and enforcing the Privacy Rule. The compliance date for most of those affected by the Rule was April 14, 2003.

Provisions of the Privacy Rule: The Privacy Rule addresses the use and disclosure of health information contained in individual

Privacy Rule affected research. The Panel continues to be concerned about these HIPAA-related barriers, she said. On behalf of the Panel, she asked that IOM conduct a study and recommend changes in HIPAA that would resolve some of these issues. She asked, "How can HIPAA be modified to address the problems for research yet retain the protections for privacy?"

After a brisk discussion among the Forum members, it was decided that this was an important subject that deserved a comprehensive initial exploration with a series of invited speakers at the next meeting of the Forum on June 16, 2006. Several Forum members emphasized that such an exploration, while it should include cancer research, should not be focused exclusively on research of one particular type or involving one particular health records—"protected health information" (PHI)—by organizations subject to the Privacy Rule—"covered entities." Covered entities include health plans, health care clearinghouses, and health care providers that transmit health information electronically. All "individually identifiable health information" held or transmitted by a covered entity is protected under the Privacy Rule and considered PHI. This includes data relating to: the individual's past, present, or future physical or mental health or condition; the provision of health care to the individual; or the past, present, or future payment for the provision of health care to the individual. Common items like name, address, birth date, and Social Security Number are included in PHI. "De-identified" health information–information that does not identify an individual or provide the means to do so—is under no disclosure restrictions. The Privacy Rule defines the circumstances under which PHI may be used or disclosed by covered entities. PHI can be used by them in the normal course of providing medical care and the necessary administrative and financial transactions. Most other uses of PHI, including under most circumstances health research, require explicit written authorization by the individual (or personal representative).

SOURCE: Adapted from NIH and OCR guidances accessed August 24, 2003 at http://privacyruleandresearch.nih.gov/pr_02.asp and http://www.hhs.gov/ocr/hipaa. Also see Glossary at the end of this Proceedings.

disease or condition. Forum members also agreed that any examination of the Privacy Rule should include concern for continuing and reliable privacy of protected health information as well as concern for the effective and efficient performance of health research. The Forum should hear presentations on the effect of the HIPAA Privacy Rule on health research of various kinds and on the protection of privacy of health information in various situations, although, clearly, given the request from the President's Cancer Panel, the emphasis would be on effects on health research.

These proceedings of a workshop presented to the National Cancer Policy Forum are the result of the Forum decision to examine the HIPAA Privacy Rule and its effects on health research and privacy. In preparation for the June meeting, the Forum invited a group of speakers balanced among those from all sectors, private academic, advocacy, industry, and public, including those who were focused on protecting the privacy of health information, those who had participated in preparation of the Privacy Rule, those who were responsible for both funding and carrying out health research, and those who had studied the Privacy Rule and recommended changes. Also, the North American Association of Central Cancer Registries carried out a short, two-question survey of its members enquiring about HIPAA Privacy Rule generated problems in cancer registry research, and the results of this brief preliminary survey were presented to the workshop. The agenda for the workshop as it actually took place is reproduced in the appendix to these proceedings. Chapter 2 includes the presentations of the invited speakers and the comments of speakers, Forum members, and others in attendance as transcribed and edited to eliminate redundancies, grammatical errors, and otherwise make them more readable. Material from PowerPoints used by speakers to support their presentations has occasionally been added to the text to clarify the speakers' messages as needed.

This workshop consumed the major part of a regularly scheduled meeting of the National Cancer Policy Forum. The Forum was established as a unit of the IOM on May 1, 2005 with support from the federal DHHS agencies, the National Cancer Institute (NCI), the Centers for Disease Control and Prevention (CDC), the Agency for Healthcare Research and Quality (AHRQ), the Food and Drug Administration (FDA), the Centers for Medicare and Medicaid Services (CMS), and the Health Resources and Services Administration (HRSA), and the private sector organizations, the American Cancer Society (ACS), the American Society of Clinical Oncology (ASCO), C-Change, and UnitedHealth Group. The Forum was a successor to the National Cancer Policy Board (1997–2005) and was designed to provide its 22 governmental, industry, academic, and other members a venue for exchanging information and presenting individual views on emerging policy issues in the nation's effort to combat cancer. Publication of these proceedings informs the Forum and, in addition, provides an opportunity to make the information and views presented and discussed at the workshop available to a wider public audience. Only what was actually communicated at the workshop is reported here without additional comment, interpretation, or analysis, although as a response to Dr. Kripke's request these proceedings might serve as an opening to additional IOM study.

REFERENCES

Reuben, SH, (Ed.) *Living Beyond Cancer: Finding a New Balance,* President's Cancer Panel, 2003 Annual Report, National Cancer Institute, National Institutes of Health, May 2004.

Reuben, SH, (Ed.) *Assessing Progress, Advancing Change,* President's Cancer Panel, 2005–2006 Annual Report, National Cancer Institute, National Institutes of Health, June 2006.

2

Prepared Presentations and Discussion

Dr. Harold Moses, Chair, National Cancer Policy Forum: This morning we open a workshop on the effects on health research of the HIPAA Privacy Rule that went into effect in April 2003. We have a number of presentations from distinguished experts from the private and public sectors that we expect will inform the IOM National Cancer Policy Forum. This workshop has been approved by the National Research Council's Governing Board Executive Committee. Workshop proceedings will be prepared as an edited transcript of the speakers' remarks, our discussion, and material presented to us during the day, and the proceedings will be published by the National Academies Press as an official IOM document. At the end of the workshop, we will have an opportunity to comment on whether there should be any IOM follow up and what form, if any, that should take. The workshop will inform us, and, importantly, it could, if further efforts are undertaken, also provide helpful input to additional IOM study.

With that, I would like to introduce Susan McAndrew from the Office for Civil Rights (OCR) in the Department of Health and Human Services. Susan, if you are ready, please proceed.

Susan McAndrew, Esq., Acting Deputy Director for Health Information Privacy, DHHS Office for Civil Rights, Information on the Privacy Rule and Health Research from the DHHS Office for Civil Rights: I want to thank the Forum for inviting OCR to make this presentation and to join in the conversation about what the effects of the HIPAA Privacy Rule have been on research operations.

There is not time to fill you in on all of the details of the HIPAA Privacy Rule. My colleague, Christina Heide, and I have been working on this Rule since 2000, and I think Christina was working on it even before then. So, this is what we have done for the past six years, and we are quite passionate about the Privacy Rule. The most I can do this morning is to highlight some general operational parameters with regard to the Privacy Rule, where we are today with regard to how the Rule interacts with research, and where we are going in the future. I will describe some of the fundamentals to keep in mind when discussing the Privacy Rule and discuss some of the basic provisions in the Rule. I also will tell you how we got where we are, what recommendations we have received since the last modifications in August of 2002, and try to respond to your request for information on complaints that we have received.

In terms of the fundamentals, there are four points. First, our purpose was to establish for the first time a uniform set of federal standards nationwide for how health plans and most health care providers should treat the identifiable health information that they receive from their patients. The Privacy Rule deals with the interaction of the consumer and the health care provider and/or the health plan for the purposes of receiving treatment and getting that treatment paid for. The impetus for HIPAA was to provide uniform transaction standards for some basic administrative and financial functions and, as the health industry back office computerized, to make sure that there were both privacy and security protections with respect to those data. So, the Privacy Rule embodies those standards. I would note now some ten years after enactment of HIPAA that we are essentially having that same debate about concerns and trade-offs as the electronic movement goes from the back-office functions into the clinical functions. What are the privacy and security provisions that are needed as the clinical side computerizes?

The second fundamental point is that because we were thinking of the consumer, our key focus is on controls for how this information on treatment, payment, and health care operations can be used and disclosed. Nonetheless, we recognize that in addition to needing this information for those functions, there are other functions—other public policy purposes— for which this information is needed. For example, we recognized health research as a national public priority for the information, and we set about finding ways to ensure the information could flow for that purpose.

The third point to keep in mind is that we deal with a limited set of entities, called covered entities, primarily health plans and health care providers, provided that they participate in electronic transactions. This will be most hospitals and large facilities and most doctors' offices, although some practitioners who deal strictly on a cash basis or provide free clinical services may be excepted. With regard to these covered entities, we tried to provide them with one set of policies in each area, and, for research, there is one set of policies, regardless of how the research is funded or whatever the other (non-privacy) rules are that apply to that research. We wanted to give a covered entity permission to use and disclose patient health information for research purposes, but within a single set of rules that apply to all research, so there would not be multiple requirements.

Whether or not the entity doing the research is itself a covered entity is a key distinction. If the entity that is doing the research is not covered by the Rule, then access to information from a covered entity is the only concern—how to obtain information needed for research from an entity that may be covered by the Rule. For those that are using health information for research and that are also covered by the Rule, the disposition of the information after obtaining it for a research purpose is also an issue. This often comes up with regard to databases and repositories. If the database or repository is outside a covered entity, the issues that have disturbed researchers are no longer a concern, and the only issue involves moving data from a covered entity to the database or repository. If the database is managed within a covered entity, then the Privacy Rule affects how that information flows out to others.

There are four channels that the Rule provides for health information to flow for research purposes. They align with the general principles of the Rule. If there is a fundamental principle of the Rule it would be that patient health information ought to be limited to the core purposes for which that consumer has come to the entity; that is, treatment, payment, and the health care operations of that entity. Otherwise, information should flow only with the individual's permission. That permission ought to be knowing and voluntary on the part of the individual. That lines up with a first principle in human research—the informed consent process. We call it authorization.

Absent treatment, payment, or health care operations, and absent the patient's permission, the Rule encourages the use of non-identifiable or de-identified information for other purposes. We did make some exceptions for certain national priority purposes, such as public health, disclosure to law enforcement, and, in some cases, research. For these limited purposes, we allow disclosure of information without the individual's knowledge or consent. In research, this requires an Institutional Review Board (IRB) or a privacy board waiver of patient authorization or permission for that disclosure.

We have carved out a few other exceptions in the research area to try to conform permissions under the Rule with other types of information that have traditionally flowed for research; this includes decedent information and more recently—in 2002—we have created what we call the limited data set. This can include dates and other detailed information, such as geographic information, about an individual, which otherwise would not have qualified as de-identified information, provided that there is a data use agreement. That conformed our rule more closely with non-IRB research—the exempt category of research.

We emphasize that the Privacy Rule does not supersede either FDA regulations on research or the Common Rule. By the same token, FDA regulations and the Common Rule do not supersede or preempt the HIPAA Privacy Rule. These regulations work within their spheres independently and jointly. So, if you are subject to both, you must comply with both. This sort of situation is not uncommon. Providers often are subject to multiple federal and state privacy schemes.

We expect a knowing and voluntary permission for research so that research will be going forward with the informed consent of the individual. We have made many changes in our authorization process to coordinate with the informed consent requirement under the Common Rule. For instance, we encouraged combination of the consent and authorization forms. We also eliminated the requirement for an expiration date, because in some cases research involves a database, and there is no time limit for residence of the protected health information in that database. Regarding revocation of authorization, we clarified what can be done with research information that has already been collected, and we accept that participation in clinical trials can be conditional on authorization for use of health information from that trial.

With regard to when the individual's permission is not needed, here we basically looked to the IRB as a trusted intermediary to make the decision on when a research project could go forward with a waiver, on the research side, of informed consent and, on the privacy side, of authorization. The alternative to an IRB would have been to leave this decision to individual covered entities. We did not feel that these entities were in a position to make waiver judgments, however, nor do I believe that it would serve research purposes to have covered entities making these decisions about the necessity for research without permission.

Our criteria for IRB waiver of HIPAA authorization (disclosure involves no more than minimal risk to privacy, research not practicable without waiver, and research not practicable without protected health information) are basically patterned from the Common Rule informed consent waiver criteria. We started with a much different list, but because we got a lot of negative feedback on that, we collapsed the list, and we constructed it more carefully to be consistent with the Common Rule criteria to ensure that the IRBs were working within a familiar realm when dealing with the privacy balances. And we tried to explain how some of these new balances would work when we take these criteria and focus them on privacy.

Finally, we dealt in the Rule with situations in which neither authorization under the Rule nor waiver of permission by an IRB would be required. These are limited situations, and they are largely based on interactions that we had with the research community about their activities that did not involve an IRB or informed consent. The first of these is the category: preparatory to research. This category is to ensure that there is sufficient access to information necessary to create a research protocol in the first place. Unfortunately, this has often been confused in some of the literature with recruitment, but it was not intended to be a recruitment tool, largely because one of the conditions is that the identifiable information accumulated cannot be taken from the covered entity.

The limited data set I would touch on only to say that this is a provision from 2002 in response to a comment from the research community. There has not been much focus on this in the literature, and I am interested in why that is. There still seem to be many questions and concerns about the stringency with which the Privacy Rule defines de-identified information. The goal of the limited data set was to provide for research purposes more robust data that are closer to comparable non-personally-identifiable data by Common Rule standards, but with the protection of a data use agreement because we do not consider this information to be de-identified. It was a way of getting more information available to the research community in a form that we thought would resolve most of the concerns about the stringency of the HIPAA de-identification standards. We have been very reluctant to lower the standard for de-identified information further, however, because we remain convinced that a lesser standard would allow protected health information to become public in all contexts, not just in research.

So, those are the basic ways that information can be used. In the Privacy Rule, we have tried to create a balance between the individual's expectations for privacy of his or her health information and the need for this information, not just for the basic purposes of health care but for other important purposes. Admittedly, we have tried to tip the balance a little in favor of the individual, not only toward control through consent and the authorization process for the use of the health information for these other purposes, but also through disclosing to the individual as much as possible how the information was used. So, the individual is informed throughout this process.

We last modified the Privacy Rule in 2002. When we did so, we included many of the provisions that I have just reviewed in response to comments that we got from the research community. We tried to make the Rule more compatible with not only the Common Rule, but what we knew about actual operating procedures in the field, while keeping true to our basic goal of making sure that we had through HIPAA a single set of rules that worked for research, not only research that was governed by the Common Rule, but research that was outside the rule—subject to the FDA or other kinds of regulations.

We have extensive guidance that we have issued in cooperation with our colleagues at NIH. I think there is probably more research advisory and technical assistance on our web site than on any other single topic—eight sets of guidance materials and hundreds of frequently asked questions (FAQs) that came out between 2003 and 2005. We are certainly very eager to know how they are doing and if they have been helpful. Since 2002, we have continued conversations about the Privacy Rule and its research provisions. We have the official comments from the Secretary's Advisory Committee on Human Research Protections, as well as recommendations from our official privacy advisory committee, the National Committee on Vital and Health Statistics.

To the extent the Forum was interested in complaints, I can report that we have had over 20,000 complaints since April of 2003. I can't give you a number on how many of those involved research. However, there have definitely been complaints involving research issues, such as concerns about calls that complainants have received from third parties. Complainants were unaware of how callers got their information, and occasionally individuals who have a particular rare condition complain of calls for a variety of purposes, such as recruitment to different research projects. They just want to be taken off the list. But, by no means is research a major complaint item for us.

Dr. Moses: Thank you very much. Are there questions?

Dr. Mark Clanton, Deputy Director, NCI: I was involved in the implementation of HIPAA rules at a health plan five or six years ago, so I am generally familiar with the Privacy Rule. Is there language that limits the protections of HIPAA for citizens that relates to certain research and identifiable information in the international context? It appears that the number of biorepositories is going to increase in countries other than the United States, and DNA or tissue data of various kinds are going to be transmitted from those repositories back into the United States for processing and analysis. I'm wondering how HIPAA applies to data that are sent to us from outside of the country.

Ms. McAndrew: The effect of the Privacy Rule is not limited to U.S. citizens. Anyone who seeks health care has HIPAA protection for their identifiable health information in a covered entity. With regard to activities overseas, our reach would extend to the entity and whether or not that entity is within the jurisdiction of the United States. If the information comes into this country and is being analyzed by an entity that is covered by HIPAA, then that entity is in possession of identifiable health information subject to HIPAA protections.

Dr. Moses: Thank you, Ms. McAndrew. Let's now proceed with the writing of the privacy rules in the Department of Health and Human Services presented by Marcy Wilder.

Marcy Wilder, Esq., Partner, Hogan and Hartson, Washington, DC, and Former Deputy General Counsel, DHHS, Writing the Privacy Rule in DHHS: I am Marcy Wilder, an attorney with the law firm of Hogan and Hartson in Washington, DC. Before joining the firm, I was the deputy general counsel at DHHS and was the lead lawyer working on the HIPAA Privacy Rule. In that capacity, I led a team of lawyers advising the 65 policy makers that were working on the Rule.

You may have been affected by the Privacy Rule, and, as you ran into trouble spots in implementing it, you probably have wondered—what was HHS thinking? I have a unique perspective as someone who worked very hard to get this Rule right and then left HHS and now has spent six years working with academic medical centers, pharmaceutical companies, technology vendors, hospitals, and others to try to implement the privacy provisions. I think it is fair to say as a regulator looking at the big picture that HHS did a lot of things right, but I think that there are also a number of places where change and improvement are needed.

HHS was seeking a balance. We were seeking to protect patient privacy and yet avoid creating undue barriers to medical research. That is true as far as it goes, but it is also true that HIPAA was not a regulation about research. Research was not a central consideration, nor the thing that got the most attention, and it was also a difficult issue. It was clear that the agency was trying to protect health information. It was clear that that information was needed by providers to treat patients and to get paid. Plans needed the information to make payments and for health care operations, to run their businesses, to make the health care system go. It was also clear that before protected health information could be used for marketing, the agency was going to require the patient to consent, to provide authorization, to give permission. The conversations about research were complicated. Research was already regulated. We were not regulating research, and although we knew that the HIPAA Privacy Rule would affect medical research, it was not clear how. So, as a more difficult conversation that was not central to the policy debate, it was put off until late in the process.

In the end, research did get a fair amount of attention, although not from people who were intimately familiar with how the research world operated. We knew about the Common Rule that for almost 25 years had regulated research privacy. We knew that IRBs determined whether research protocols contained provisions adequate to protect the privacy of participants and to maintain the confidentiality of data. Many made the argument that provisions were already in place to protect the privacy of participants in research. But as we talked to researchers and looked at the comments we were receiving, we had the impression that privacy was not a central concern for IRBs. Nobody was identifying major problems, but privacy wasn't a focus, and there seemed to be a need to ensure that health information was given protection consistent with the heightened attention required by HIPAA.

HIPAA is independent of the Common Rule and regulates not research itself but access by researchers to protected health information in covered entities. Policy makers aimed for consistency with the Common Rule and the FDA research rules, but certainly didn't harmonize the research regulatory framework. Maybe harmonization is something we will talk about: whether or not it is a good idea or what needs to be done to achieve it. At the time of the 2000 rulemaking, however, comments received by HHS mostly did not propose alternatives but instead focused on the negative impact privacy protections would have on health care and medical research. Usually, in a complicated rulemaking, stakeholders with diverse views come to the table. Everybody is pretty familiar with what you are trying to do, and they have points of view. "Don't do it this way." "Do it this way." "This is a very bad idea." "That just might work." But for the HIPAA Privacy Rule, the comments tended to be—and from a number of sectors—what I think of as the "not doable" chorus, which leaves the regulator to make a decision whether it is truly not doable or whether a best efforts attempt needs to be made.

After the initial implementation of the Rule, it became clear there were instances where the Rule was impeding research, and there were aggressive advocacy efforts for changes. As a result, in the 2002 final rule HHS added new provisions such as the limited data set provisions, an alternative for accounting of disclosures, and simplified criteria for research authorization waivers. So, there were some fixes at that time, but over the past three or four years since then, it has become evident that more change is needed.

I think part of the frustration that researchers are experiencing is due to the fact that much of the voluminous guidance on research and HIPAA does a good job of explicating what is in the Rule which helps people better implement what is there. But it does not, however, and maybe shouldn't, go to some of the issues that actually need fixing, that is, where the problem is not misunderstanding or overzealous compliance, but rather intrinsic to the Rule requiring an actual regulatory change. Because research wasn't a central concern of the rulemaking, in part because there was not then an experience base of efforts to apply aggressive privacy protections in the research context, there remain some issues that need further attention.

For example, there are some areas where the burdens on research are heavy and the privacy benefits slim. One that is faced largely by academic medical centers is the accounting for disclosures in research being conducted pursuant to an IRB waiver. In large institutions with many protocols, investigators may access records held by a covered entity under an IRB waiver, many of which ultimately will not be used in the research. Every paper record examined means a disclosure form to fill out; every electronic record examined means a system, a screen, to go through for access, and a click to record that use of the record. These are processes that (given the numbers of research projects, investigators, and potential research subjects) require very substantial time and dollar resources to create and follow for both the researcher and the management of the entities involved. Accounting for record access is not necessarily bad, but when you look at the cost/benefit analysis of the accounting for disclosure for IRB-approved research, it is very questionable whether there are privacy benefits to the patient or participant commensurate with the costs to the research and health care enterprise. I note this especially in view of the fact that very few participants or patients ever request an accounting for disclosure. Moreover, even if there was a measurable benefit to the patient in keeping track of these kinds of disclosures, on balance, it likely would not justify the resources expended.

The second area that needs attention involves situations where the Privacy and Common Rule diverge, and research suffers as a result of our failure to harmonize the two frameworks. For example, under the Common Rule, investigators can ask for informed consent for use of information in future unspecified research (sometimes bounded by type, such as cancer research, sometimes not) but under the parallel HIPAA authorization requirement, investigators may get permission only for the use of protected health information for a specific identified research project. The right of participants to consent to the use of their data in future unspecified research was taken away by the Privacy Rule. There are workarounds for this, but the lack of elegance in the workarounds reflects the fundamental tension between HIPAA and the Common Rule. The policy question of to what extent individuals should be able to consent to the use of their information for future research ought to be answered and guidance provided.

Another small example and one that probably should be fixed and can be easily fixed involves translation of consent and authorization into an unanticipated foreign language. The Common Rule has a relatively easy process for obtaining informed consent when an unanticipated need for a translation arises. The process involves a summary consent form in the participants language, an oral translation of the full form, and an "oral informed" consent with documentation. The Privacy Rule does not have a parallel process.

The last example, which I think is an enormous issue that deserves more attention, involves the new federal standard for de-identification of health information that was created by the Privacy Rule. There has been a lot of back and forth as to whether it is too narrow or whether the statistician method of de-identification is enough of an alternative. Can it be made to work better and be more available? And are the liability burdens of de-identifying data properly distributed? Problems arise when an investigator would like to use de-identified information, but the research does not go forward because the covered entity that has the information either does not have the motivation to de-identify, does not want to spend the money to de-identify, or is worried about complaints and liability for non-compliance with the Rule's de-identification requirements. Is there some other way to distribute those burdens that will protect privacy but remove what in some areas is a significant barrier to important research?

This has been a topic of discussion from the beginning. I think HHS went a long way in addressing it by adding the provisions for the use of limited data sets and by providing the statistician method of de-identification. But I think more needs to be done. On the other hand, I hope everybody was sensitive to OCR's concerns that, although there may be a case for making this information available with less stringent standards, including dates and zip codes, for instance, there is a real concern that a lesser standard will risk leaking health information beyond the research setting.

When advocating change, there must first be a dialogue that takes the concerns of the regulators into consideration. Issues must be clearly identified, and policy alternatives must be developed and aggressively promoted. You can't fight something with nothing. We will need concrete examples of how research is affected and alternatives that address the concerns that the regulators have expressed. If not, the issues will sound too hard to the ears of the regulator, and nothing may be done.

Second, we need ally agencies within HHS. I think there will be many, because many HHS agencies are involved in HIPAA, involved in research. There are many important HHS agencies that are affected by HIPAA research privacy provisions: everything from NIH research, CMS Pay-for-Performance efforts, all the efforts to promote health information technology, and much that is going on at the FDA and AHRQ. The agencies involved include the Office for Civil Rights, the National Institutes of Health (NIH), the Food and Drug Administration (FDA), the Agency for Healthcare Research and Quality (AHRQ), the Centers for Medicare and Medicaid Services (CMS), the Office of E-Health Standards and Services, and the Office of the National Coordinator of Health Information Technology. They have all encountered challenges associated with implementing the research provisions of the Privacy Rule. My guess is there are already internal conversations about this, and engaging the right allies within HHS will be important to any effort to make changes.

So, the bottom line is, yes there are challenges. Yes, some of them will require changes or perhaps more guidance. That will need to be determined, but the research rules can be modified. Advisory committees, Congress, and agencies within HHS itself have recognized that the HIPAA Privacy Rule research provisions need improvement. The IOM recommendations will matter.

Dr. Moses: Thank you. We do have time for questions.

Dr. Peter Bach, Senior Advisor to the Administrator, CMS: Could you talk a little more about the statistician method?

Ms. Wilder: There are two ways to de-identify information under HIPAA. One is the safe harbor, where you have to remove 18 identifiers, including dates of service, birth dates, as well as zip codes. The statistician method is an alternative whereby you can engage a qualified statistician to analyze a data set and make a determination that the likelihood of re-identification is very small. If you get that statistician certification, then the data set is considered de-identified under the regulation. Those certifications are only as good as the assumptions on which they are based. So, usually in the certification there will be a set of assumptions—assuming the specified data elements are the only data fields, that certain policies are in place, and that contractual restrictions are in place. In using the data set the recipient needs to be careful to stay within the bounds of the certification.

Dr. Bach: How frequently is the statistician method used? Has it been externally validated? How much oversight is there at the federal level or by institutional IRBs or others?

Ms. Wilder: There are a handful of statisticians who provide this service, not a lot. They are hard to find. It is being used increasingly in the past year and a half, not because of a lot more statisticians, just increased use of the method. There is no oversight of the use of that methodology.

Dr. Bach: Other than a Ph.D. in statistics, do the statisticians have any special training or qualifications or Common Rule orientation.

Ms. Wilder: Sometimes they do and sometimes they don't. A lot of the large data companies, for example, are using the statistician method, but it is not something that has been looked at closely.

Dr. Thomas Burish, Provost, Notre Dame: My question is about when HIPAA applies. I thought Ms. McAndrew said if a practice takes cash only, or if it provides services free of charge, then the Rule doesn't apply. I presume that if the practice accepts insurance payments, however, then it doesn't matter what other methods of payment it accepts—you have to follow HIPAA. So, if an entity has multiple payment schemes, including insurance as one of them, then HIPAA applies. Is that correct?

Ms. McAndrew: If you are a provider, you are covered by the Rule if you engage in one of the transactions for which HIPAA has a standard, and those are basically administrative and financial standards. We tend to talk about billing as a short cut to explain the kinds of providers that are covered by HIPAA. Basically, if you bill electronically, for instance, Medicare or any of the private payers, and you do that billing process electronically, you are covered by HIPAA.

Dr. Burish: You are a free clinic at an educational institution. You don't charge at all. The clinic is just for training purposes for students—no cash, no billing. It's not covered?

Ms. McAndrew: If you don't have any electronic billing, if you don't do eligibility because you don't bill a private insurance company, then, no, you are likely not covered.

Dr. David Parkinson, Senior Vice President, Oncology Research and Development, Biogen IDEC: How does that fit with your answer to Dr. Clanton? Foreign patients, to my knowledge, are not being billed by American entities.

Ms. McAndrew: If your patient is covered by Blue Cross/Blue Shield and you come to me, and I send your bill off electronically to Blue Cross/Blue Shield, I am a covered entity. Then, if you come in, and I give you essentially pro bono services, free services, because I have billed electronically, I am a covered entity and your information, even though you are a non-paying customer is covered. So, the response was—if the information comes in to a covered entity, that information is covered regardless of whether you are a citizen or not.

Dr. Parkinson: But you realize as a global sponsor the kinds of problems this gives us, because then we have to abide by HIPAA rules on the collection of the information, right? And the French usually are not that cooperative.

Ms. McAndrew: We'll need to come back to that. I'm not sure that's correct.

Dr. Ralph Coates, Associate Director for Science, Division of Cancer Prevention and Control, CDC: And if that international information went to researchers but not a covered entity, then HIPAA would not apply?

Dr. Bach: The same as if you are injecting Botox in a salon as a licensed physician just to get cash.

Dr. Moses: Let's move on to Paul Feldman from the Health Privacy Project.

Paul Feldman, Deputy Director, Health Privacy Project, Raising Public Awareness of the Importance of Health Privacy: I am happy to be here and among esteemed researchers and colleagues. Much of what I was going to say has already been covered by the previous speakers which I thought might happen. So, that is great. I want to start with the lead, which is that we have a common understanding here; that there is a balance—we all want biomedical and other research to continue with due speed and as much effectiveness as possible. This is not an adversarial relationship. We also are all in this together, and in fact, to make the obvious point, we are all patients and consumers of health care services. Our medical privacy is important to all of us. So, I want to start there.

I want to tell a couple of personal stories quickly to kind of set the framework for my comments. Soon after I came to D.C. to take another job in policy and advocacy, I was fortunate enough to be at a meeting with Tony Fauci. He had to leave early for another gig, and I ran out of the meeting to jump into the elevator with him because in my world Tony Fauci is Brad Pitt. His work has been incredibly important to me, and his ability to negotiate an incredibly difficult terrain is something that I hold very dear.

I am a person living with AIDS, and if anyone understands the value of biomedical research, it is I. I have been living with it from the very beginning, having had a frozen blood sample before there was HIV, and I am one of the lucky ones obviously. I am a survivor. Probably some of you in this room, and certainly many of your colleagues, have been involved in those research efforts and, of course, I owe you my life, in fact. I think that there are others among us, who can tell a similar story. We are all in this together, and we must be sure not to impede research, and we must be sure to protect privacy. So, as we go on today and perhaps have an opportunity to debate some of the points (I have some responses to some of the things that Marcy Wilder said, for example), it will be in the spirit of getting the job done and in the spirit of protecting the balance.

To make this real, Marcy knows that part of these presentations from our perspective always include some of this information, I want to tell you a couple of stories. I doubt I need to go through the VA privacy breach story. I sat in mark-ups yesterday for health IT bills in both Energy and Commerce and Ways and Means Committees, and various members mentioned the VA breach at least five times. It was getting annoying, even to me. Meanwhile, during the mark-up, I happened to be flipping through *The New York Times,* and on page C13, not the front page or even the front page of the business or circuit section, there was a little item about AIG, one of the biggest insurers in the nation, suffering the theft from "one of its Midwest offices" of nearly a million records containing identifiable personal information including "fragments of medical information." We are in a very dangerous place right now, and we need to protect the data, but we also need to protect and improve consumer confidence in the health care system and by extension, I would argue, the research community. I believe that most individuals engage with the research community as an extension of health care, which I think is a useful framework to use when analyzing the effects of data breaches and unwanted disclosures of personal information.

Then there's another story I have to share. I want to make sure that everybody knows the story of the oncologist, who had cancer and decided that his pathology slides were useful for the advancement of a conversation—I don't have the details on what kind of cancer or what kind of conversation. He later discovers that his slide has been identified and put in a database with his name on it. This was not his intention. It happened. Mistakes happen. So, this is the environment that patients walk into, and we need to address it. We need to be very careful to foster trust, which is what this is about. These things happen. There is no system available, paper-based or electronic, which will guarantee that there are no breaches, that there are no mistakes. Nobody is expecting that. What we are expecting is that we all have due diligence to keep moving on to improve, to improve, to improve.

Stories like these are on our web site, by the way. We have medical privacy stories, our horror stories we call them. I am in the process of actually getting them updated because I saw that there were some gaps, but there is an incredible litany of scary things that you would not like to have happen to you or your loved ones. So, I wanted to walk through why we care about privacy and security of the data. Why do patients care so much? I think it bears walking through an example.

We will talk just for a minute about HIV. One of the headlines that we are all familiar with is the changing face of the epidemic, that it has moved into different communities. We all know the story. It began as a white, gay, male thing and quickly moved on. It took a long time for people to be able to talk about the changing face of the epidemic. This year, around half of new infections, 40,000 new infections in this country, will be found in men who have sex with men. Somewhere between a third and a half of those will be found in men who have sex with men who are under 25 years old. We also know the statistic that the majority of new infections are found among African Americans, and the plurality among people from communities of color. This country just passed 11 or 12 anti-gay marriage amendments in 2004 with vigor and any number of hateful referenda and legislation. This is a brew for stigma and avoidance of care and avoidance of sharing complete information with a provider. So what are you going to do as a young gay man? Or you are an old, gay man, like me, and you are not out. Are you going to go to your regular doctor to talk about the mole whose size has changed? Maybe. Maybe not. You might go to another doctor.

The California Health Care Foundation commissioned Forrester Research to do an opinion study in 2005 on national consumer health privacy following up on their benchmark 1999 study. They found that consumers remained concerned about the privacy of their personal health information. Two-thirds of respondents were somewhat or very concerned about the privacy of their personal health information. The number is greater among racial and ethnic minorities, nearly three-quarters. The other important fact is that privacy protecting behaviors persist despite changes in the environment with the advent of HIPAA and the Privacy Rule. About one in eight individuals does something adverse to care or treatment in an attempt, sometimes successful, sometimes not, to protect privacy. So, we continue to be concerned.

But there is good news. Just over half of respondents believe that they have a duty to share their personal health information for the advancement of science. I would argue that that number increases with belief that their information is safe. So, as we do our work, I think it is useful to remember that we do have a prize to keep our eyes on, and it is fostering trust that encourages seeking full health care and treatment and participating in research.

I wanted to talk for a minute or two about our understanding of the Privacy Rule in general. It is pretty clear, from the research that we have looked at and the anecdotes that we hear, that many, many of the problems that are reported with the conduction of studies or preparatory research are the result of misunderstanding of the existing privacy regulation.

Let me give you a couple of examples. IRBs believe they have no authority to approve alterations to or waivers of authorization for protocols not subject to the Common Rule. They do. That is the answer. Second and subsequent sites of multi-site trials won't accept the IRB approval of waiver from the first IRB, but they can. The notion that it is burdensome to engage in multi-site trials because of a requirement for multiple IRB approvals of waivers is incorrect. The first IRB waiver does the job. IRBs often refuse to rely on this. When using the statistician method or otherwise engaging in de-identification of data, covered entities are concerned for liability and good faith reasons about doing it correctly, that it is not being done properly and that individuals may have their privacy compromised, their information exposed. So, in any event, they don't do it. This is something that can be cured with more guidance. I know there is already voluminous guidance—it is correct that on the OCR site, the research information is the most robust—but I believe we need to advocate for additional funding going to OCR to enable more education, more outreach, and more investigation of what these misunderstandings are, so that they can be remedied with knowledge.

I expect we are going to hear a lot today about specific problems, and I am glad to hear them, and I want to learn from this day so that I can, first, better understand researchers' issues and then help craft some solutions. One of the things that we will talk about is a consent bias, the notion that engaging in consent plus authorization not only is burdensome, but it discourages participation in studies. I think there is evidence to show that there is some truth to that, yet at the same time we don't study privacy bias; what is the relationship between confidence in the privacy of personal information and willingness to engage in research? As we discuss what works and doesn't work and needs to be changed, this is something that needs further study and discussion among us.

I have a friend who is a career employee at the FDA, and when I came to town, I called her up. She said to me, you know, the most important day as I understand it in the history of the FDA was the day that Act Up closed us down, or shut the doors anyway. It was called "Storm the FDA." It changed what we did, the way that we approve drugs, the speed at which we do it. It was an engagement with consumers, with activists, that helped make that happen, working with researchers, balancing the need for speed and the need for complete research.

I think that as we enter into our conversations, if we treat patient privacy and effective and efficient research as oppositional, that is a recipe for disaster. We have to change the paradigm and walk in wanting to get the job done. I am here today because I want to help with this, and I hope that this is simply the opening of a long conversation. If a change is needed, then we should talk about that.

De-identification of data keeps coming up. As a person living with AIDS, when I walk into my infectious disease doc every three months for my blood draws, and I have a ten minute conversation, occasionally we will talk about daily versus twice daily dosing. Imagine a future with robust health information technology that has built into it from the beginning effective privacy and security measures so that when I report that my daily dosing of Viramune® is working, that that goes into the system. That is available and now no one ever needs to know that it is me taking the Viramune®, do they? They probably need to know my age and some other characteristics, perhaps the three digit zip code so that they can get some sense of what the practice is regionally, who knows. I am not the researcher.

Imagine a future, then, where we can develop good practice standards and suggest where evidence-based research would support these findings based on the data element that is collected. If n is large enough, as I understand it, then looking at a single datum within a group of populations starts to be meaningful. We can move beyond the practice group, which I think continues to need to exist, and be able to use this information for a common benefit.

Dr. Moses: Thank you, Paul. Do we have questions, comments?

Dr. William Robinson, Director, Office of Minority Health and Health Disparities, HRSA: I have one comment, and this follows up in part to what was said earlier about this becoming a part of a broader IOM agenda. First of all, Paul, the comments that you were making were very important to me. Tens of millions of people have no idea what HIPAA is about. It is going to be critically important if the sort of thing that occurred with the VA data happens again and affects the common ordinary everyday person who is not tied to a system like the DOD or the VA, and people begin to perceive of themselves being in personal jeopardy. It is going to really set back a number of initiatives which the research community is attempting to foster.

Paul, you talked about people living with AIDS. Think about what this country has just gone through recently with regard to immigration and the numbers of people who we are hoping will join the health care system so that we can treat some of their current problems. We have so much at stake that is going to depend on people having confidence in the system to provide good quality care and maintain their confidentiality. This applies to all of us, whether natural citizens, or immigrants, legal or illegal.

Some of us know that HIPAA is more than just signing a note when you go to the doctor's office saying it is okay to take control of my records and that you will keep them confidential. Many, if not most people basically don't know anything beyond that. To the degree that the media and others can be encouraged by IOM to engage this issue, to make sure that people are more aware of what the system is about, that is going to help us in the long run. There are so many people who have no idea what HIPAA is about and what the implications are. If one major negative headline appears, I think the impact is going to really be detrimental to not just the research community, but also to anybody who is interested in the handling of medical records.

Mr. Feldman: Thank you for your comment, because it raises another important point: meaningful enforcement. There have been 20,000 complaints to OCR since April of 2003, but not a single civil penalty assessed. On top of that, by the way, an individual has no private right of action under HIPAA to remedy harm caused by a breach of medical privacy, none. So, we have some problems already, and I think that the event that we don't want to have happen will happen sooner or later. Now, it may affect millions of folks or it may be a high profile event affecting celebrities. We might have the Rock Hudson of medical privacy coming down the pike. The issue is not that it happens. It is how we respond. It is that we have meaningful enforcement and a system that understands and acknowledges the harm that has been caused and seeks to make people whole. You can't unring the bell. Right? But you can acknowledge and attempt to ameliorate what has happened.

Thomas Kean, Executive Director, C-Change: I really appreciate both Bill's and Paul's comments, but obviously this whole discussion about HIPAA and privacy is occurring in the context of a much larger, all encompassing societal privacy discussion right now. This is very messy and very confusing, and so in our attempts to think about how we are going to educate consumers or how we are going to increase the level of understanding, we have to do it in the bigger context of where we are with privacy. I know that is very clear to everybody, but it keeps getting shunted off to the side. As an example of that, I am one of the presumably 26 1/2 million veterans who just got notified of the VA data breach. Yet I have no clue what my risk is. I have no clue what precisely was disclosed or where to go with that issue.

Mr. Feldman: One of my issues with Secretary Nicholson is that the notice did not include the fact that medical information was included in the breach, which I find insulting, in fact.

Dr. Moses: Thank you. I think it is time to move on to Roberta Ness from the University of Pittsburgh, who is chair of the Policy Committee of the American College of Epidemiology.

Dr. Roberta Ness, Chair of the Policy Committee, American College of Epidemiology, Chair and Professor of Epidemiology, and Director of Cancer Epidemiology, University of Pittsburgh, Epidemiological Research and the Privacy Rule: I am a medical epidemiologist and interim dean of the School of Public Health, chair of the Department of Epidemiology at the University of Pittsburgh, but I am speaking today on behalf of the

American College of Epidemiology, which has weighed in on the HIPAA issue on several occasions.

I want to focus on something that is just a little bit different, but, obviously, very related to what we have heard so far this morning. That is variability in the interpretation of the HIPAA Privacy Rule as it applies to research. I wanted to start with two beliefs that I have, just so that you understand where I am coming from, and they are probably not very different from beliefs that others in this room share. One is that research really can lead to the saving of human lives. The second is that researchers fundamentally believe in and are engaged in protecting confidentiality as much as is possible, because they fundamentally understand exactly what Paul Feldman was just saying, that without the protection of confidentiality, there will be no trust in research and, therefore, we will be unable to conduct research.

So, those are the two planks that I start from. The question, of course, that we are engaged in addressing today, and that hopefully IOM will take up in more depth in the future, is whether HIPAA has effectively helped that balance between the need to do research and the need to protect confidentiality. I would love to bring to you today some data. In fact, there have been some data collected. I was pleased to see that you heard from Susan Ehringhaus (Associate Counsel at the Association of American Medical Colleges, AAMC) at the Forum's last meeting, and therefore you have seen probably almost the only data that have been collected to date. But I think we are all aware that those data were effectively biased, because it was a select group of individuals who responded to that survey. So, I don't want to tell you that we really know very much about the way in which HIPAA has been affecting the research community.

I am going to spend my time today doing what no self-respecting epidemiologist would ever do; I am going to tell you stories, because that is really all I have. To begin with an overview, HIPAA is interpreted by local IRBs, as you know. The outcome of that is tremendous variability, which results, I believe, in less protection to human subjects. I will tell you why I say that. And certainly it is a risk to science.

I have no idea why HIPAA was interpreted so variably at these various institutions. This is simply how it is. Here is one extreme. The Karmonas Hospital in Detroit runs the SEER Cancer Registry in that area. Karmonas research staff are employed as SEER registrars, and cancer cases are identified for research purposes at the time of registry identification by the staff. Physicians are only contacted as a courtesy. In other words, they don't even need to be contacted in order to move from the cancer registry to requesting that an individual be a participant in research.

Yale received a waiver to identify potential cancer cases from medical records without authorization on the basis of convincing the IRB that, indeed, this protocol was minimum risk and involved research that could not be done without the waiver. The physicians in this institution must be notified and must agree that the patient be contacted for research before the contact can be made, but thereafter the research staff goes ahead and contacts the subject. In many cases, the physician consents or agreements consist of a letter that says any of my patients can be involved in this research protocol. So, that is kind of in the middle.

Now, some of you may not be aware that there has been some news reporting on this issue. HIPAA really came on line in January of 2003. About 18 months later, an article appeared in Science, the byline of which was that this is a complicated new regulation potentially hindering a broad swath of science, from population-based science to genetic studies to tissue repositories. In that particular news article, Jocelyn Kaiser reported that for outcomes research, in many cases, the Privacy Rule is limiting the ability to do outcome studies based on medical records. In that regard, many of us have seen the smaller hospitals and community hospitals just dropping out of protocols altogether. They are simply saying they have no idea what their legal liability is; they don't have the infrastructure to assess, from an IRB perspective or from a legal perspective, what their involvement in these research protocols means in the era of HIPAA and, so, therefore, they are just not going to be involved in research anymore.

With respect to pathology, there has been an enormous amount of confusion. At some institutions subjects must be recontacted for each study using stored tissues, in some cases almost independent of whether those tissues are de-identified consistent with HIPAA protocols. Again, I am just telling you what is happening. Family history and family studies have been tremendously difficult under the Privacy Rule. This, of course, started even before HIPAA, obviously, with the case in Virginia, but there has been a lot of difficulty on the part of IRBs figuring out how genetic data or how family history information should be handled.

The next news report comes from *The San Francisco Chronicle* in September of 2004, about a year after implementation of the Rule. This was Sabin Russell's report of a major effect on cancer reporting and particularly on case control studies done in the State of California. The California Cancer Registry was unclear about how to interpret the HIPAA guidelines and, therefore, for a period of some months, simply closed down rapid case reporting to the University of California system. Researchers within the University of California system that were involved in case control studies requiring rapid case reporting were unable then to access the SEER registry and were unable to recruit subjects through what had been their major source. Now, fortunately after some discussion of lawsuits and such, University of California lawyers were eventually able to negotiate a waiver with the California Cancer Registry System and to my knowledge then things were worked out. But there was this period of time when the system was closed down.

International registries have definitely suffered delays. We have heard that for multi-institutional protocols, they will go through multiple IRBs, and because each IRB variably interprets both Common Rule and now HIPAA guidelines, it has become really a nightmare to do these protocols and that has been particularly true for international studies. Of course, the reason for that is that many of the U.S. hospitals have refused to divulge the needed patient information.

I agree that what Paul Feldman said is true. Under HIPAA guidance, it is possible for other IRBs to simply accept a previous IRB's approval of a HIPAA waiver. But that is just not the way that IRBs work. Each IRB feels that it bears a responsibility, and I have personally had conversations with IRBs at other institutions and been reminded that they control the local agenda. Their position is, don't tell us what to do—period.

Then there was a follow-up story in *Science*, which is noteworthy because it is so recent (March 17, 2006). One of the questions has been whether a lot of the variability was just a bump in the road; that is to say, nobody really knew how to interpret this new regulation. People needed additional guidance, but we have gotten over it, and things are really fine now. I think that this report because it is so recent, indicates that variability remains. There still is a lot of difficulty and challenge involved. This was primarily the story of the Minnesota heart study, which is a 25 year study that has brought us an enormous amount of population-based data on cardiovascular risk. The study reviews medical records from hospitals throughout the Minneapolis area. Identifiers, such as a social security number, are required to match hospital records and death records. Minnesota's privacy law requires recently, in good part because of HIPAA, each patient to be contacted for permission each time one of those linkages is made. As you can imagine, the response rate, going from an opportunity to make those linkages without consent versus the new requirement for consent each time, is very, very, very markedly different.

That same article reported a University of Michigan telephone survey in which written authorization before each call was required. It has been reported in other studies that when there is a need for this kind of double permission consent rates plummet from 96 percent to 34 percent. So, these Michigan researchers were really up against a great challenge.

I want to tell you a story from my own institution, which is unfortunately probably one of the only instances of real time-related data. The University of Pittsburgh, when HIPAA regulation began, decided there would be no waivers of authorization under any circumstances, because they could not be convinced there was no risk or that a waiver was absolutely necessary to do the research. As smart individuals, we were to find a way despite not having a waiver. We had a very large case control study of ovarian cancer. The identification of those cancer cases then had to come from the individual treating physician which meant that for every patient that we wanted to enroll in case control studies, we had to go to the physician for permission each time. Well, you know, physicians are very busy. That new road block halved our consent rate. That was one example.

The other example was a cohort study that was looking at preeclampsia, a disease that occurs during pregnancy. The only way that we could recruit these subjects into our ongoing cohort study after HIPAA was to persuade each patient to enroll in a registry, which is a way that investigators have been getting blanket use of medical records. The problem, of course, is getting women to enroll in the registry. Let's actually talk about the logistics of that. On her first pregnancy visit, a woman is confronted with a thick stack of paper, right? She has all this medical documentation that she needs to fill out. She needs to understand all of her insurance. She needs to understand what is going to happen throughout the whole pregnancy; and buried in all that is this HIPAA compliant registry.

If she signs it, she has absolutely no idea what she signed, and if she doesn't sign it, which frequently happens, it is because she is completely overwhelmed. After awhile she starts asking if each piece of paper is absolutely necessary. So, in fact, only about 35 percent of our patients were signing up for the registry. We were losing two-thirds right up front.

From 1998 to 2002, this cohort study (which has been refunded three times from the National Institutes of Health) had been ongoing, and we were enrolling about ten pregnant women per week. From January to April 2003, our IRB shut us down completely as HIPAA came on line, because they had absolutely no idea what to do under the Privacy Rule. So, we were shut down for four months. After we came back on line using the registry system, we were only able to enroll five patients per week—basically cut in half in terms of our enrollment.

It has been estimated by DHHS for the purposes of the regulation that the cost of HIPAA requirements for research will be about $600 million over the ten years from 2003–2012, that is, the cost of implementation at the institutional level. Clearly, HIPAA is causing researchers to revise or even avoid certain types of studies, particularly population-based studies. I would really underscore that, because my strong belief as an epidemiologist is that HIPAA does not have a really major impact on the clinician doing research on his or her own patients. That clinician is the covered entity, and it is really not difficult in that circumstance to negotiate the system. What is extremely difficult to negotiate is the capture of every patient with a particular diagnosis within a particular region, because then you are talking about multiple clinicians, multiple covered entities, and multiple institutions. You can see how extraordinarily complex this becomes. At the same time, though, population-based research is the gold standard. Those studies are the most unbiased studies that give us the best information about what is really going on.

There have been attempts to modify HIPAA. The AAMC, as you heard from Susan Ehringhaus, urged—and this is obviously the most extreme possibility—that research already approved under the Common Rule be exempt from HIPAA. In addition, they supported the Secretary's Advisory Committee on Human Research Protections (SACHRP) recommendations, which you are going to be hearing more about, and so I am not going to go into detail about those. But they were a series of recommendations proposing that, if research isn't going to be exempt, there be some ways to harmonize the Common Rule and HIPAA and some ways to do away with some of the more onerous requirements.

So,—moving from these very specific stories to what I think are some of the underlying issues—the IRBs are in a difficult position; on the one hand they are protectors of human subjects, but on the other hand, they are a service organization that is ensuring that informed consent can take place and that research can go on. That really is the duality and that really is the tension we are talking about.

Some of the specific underlying problems are: who is the covered entity? For example, I am in a school of public health which is part of the University of Pittsburgh system, but we do not see patients. Are we part of the covered entity? Although, in some institutions, the school of public health is a part of a covered entity, at the University of Pittsburgh, we are not. This gives you a sense of how extreme and fundamental this variability is.

The second broader issue: are we talking about confidentiality being protected or about the opportunity to learn about research being infringed? The reason I say that is because I believe that under HIPAA there really has been less of an opportunity, for example, for AIDS patients to learn about new protocols because of these pre-regulations about how researchers can get access to people to let them know about research. You can't even tell a subject that there is a research protocol that might be appropriate and worthwhile for them until you have, for instance, at our institution gone through the treating physician. That seems paternalism to an extreme.

I also mentioned the complexity of the consent documents. I really believe they detract from a full understanding of what subjects are getting themselves into. In many institutions now the Common Rule IRB document and the HIPAA document are separate and go on for pages and pages, and so there are really two separate consenting procedures that need to occur, and they are quite involved.

It seems clear from the stories that I just told you, that in some cases—and how widespread this is, we really don't know—there have been limitations on important types of research, chart reviews, retrospective cohort studies, population-based case control studies, multi-center studies. Ultimately, this means that the Privacy Rule is hampering the competitiveness of U.S. science. There is also, as many of you know now, a European rule which in many ways parallels HIPAA and aspects of the Common Rule. There are, however, still societies in which many of these issues are much better accepted by the population, and, in fact, where this balance between confidentiality and research is such that research far outweighs the kind of confidentiality concerns we have been talking about.

Scandinavian countries are an excellent example of that, and many American researchers are now collaborating with Denmark, Norway, or Sweden because we can't collect the data ourselves that is so beautifully collected in those countries. But what does that say about the hegemony of U.S. research in the future. There is no question that the Privacy Rule is heightening the potential for what epidemiologists call ascertainment bias. That means that only a part of the population is joining studies, and that bias can distort our understanding of health.

To summarize, some of the issues that are fundamental and very variably interpreted are: who is part of the covered entity? How do we streamline and harmonize the Privacy Rule with the Common Rule? What are appropriate parameters for allowing a waiver? How is HIPAA impeding research? And, fundamentally, is HIPAA actually protecting individual privacy with respect to research? We know that patients are concerned, but we really don't know whether HIPAA has brought us any advantages along with the problems. Should HIPAA apply to research, since research was not central when HIPAA regulations were evolving? Should research, which is already covered under IRBs through the Common Rule, be subject to these additional regulations?

Dr. Moses: Thank you, Roberta. We have time for maybe a couple of questions.

Arthur Holden, Senior Vice President, Illumina, Chairman, DMD Translational Research Consortium and Pharmaceutical Biomedical Research Consortium: May I ask two clarifying questions? Relative to the decline in patients going into your Pittsburgh registry, how much of that do you feel was because of the incremental complexity of HIPAA requirements—or just the complexity of working with the doctors and coordinating with them and getting their compliance—was it a mix or was one more important?

Dr. Ness: Absolutely a mix.

Mr. Holden: So, it is both.

Dr. Ness: Absolutely. Part of it is typically not physicians; staff don't really understand it when questions arise that kind of say, well, that is not as important as these other documents you are signing.

Mr. Holden: Second question. In international activities, do you see countries that have a single payor government system being those that facilitate and are able to strike that balance between control of information versus participation and research speed. Examples that you highlighted were fundamentally simple, much less diverse systems than we have in the United States.

Dr. Ness: I don't think that is an easy question. I would say that is really complex. Countries like the U.K. that is essentially a single payor system country have been pretty concerned about confidentiality and have put in place a relatively rigorous set of guidelines; whereas, other countries, particularly Scandinavian countries, have really not or at least have interpreted them differently. I think there is a lot of variability.

Dr. Parkinson: I can comment. The big problem is variability. One can adapt. No one is against privacy. You can adapt to any set of rules. What is hard to adapt to is that every single covered entity in the entire United States is interpreting things differently and variably over time. In a world where we are increasingly trying to link patients with tissues, the impossibility of doing that in this country is a tragedy, and it is a huge impediment in cancer research to trying to move to the next level of cancer investigation, in my opinion.

So, with respect to other countries, Europe is complex. Different countries interpret differently—but, again, one can adapt as long as the rules are consistent within a certain region—I am not arguing for complexity, but I am arguing for some sort of consistency and homogeneity, and then one can adapt to the rules.

Dr. Clanton: I just had a follow-on question and comment. You did a beautiful job describing the variable implementation of HIPAA rules, and I think the implementations are variable because of the uncertainty about what is truly acceptable.

My question is, would a HIPAA certification, similar to those of NCQA or the Joint Commission, allow a more standard approach to implementation? For example, we didn't actually get a straightforward answer to the question of whether a clinic that provided 100 percent free care would be outside HIPAA. It might help if there were a certification of some sort that said if, in fact, you have a hundred percent compliance with non-billing, you are okay.

Dr. Ness: My own personal feeling is consistent with what Marcy Wilder said. I think that some of what is going on quite clearly is a lack of understanding of the Rule, and in that case certification, or certainly a clearer in-servicing of IRB committees, would be very useful. But, as Marcy said, there are some elements of the Rule, some situations, in which there really does need to be more harmonization of the Privacy Rule with the Common Rule. Again, I will not try to preempt this, but I think that the SACHRP recommendations are quite clear in this regard. So, there are some things that need to be fixed, but in addition to that, there is a great deal more understanding that needs to be conveyed.

Mr. Holden: To build on Dr. Clanton's point, which I think is an important one, particularly relative to Bill Robinson's point on education of consumers, for five years I worked with IRBs in major academic research centers to put in infrastructures to aggregate patient data, including genetic data, to do whole genome types of research, new cutting edge research that would use the advanced tools available to us. In situation after situation, IRBs would be saying this is the help we need to do what we need to do, but the institution would not implement, was not motivated to implement. It was not a research priority. So, along with certification, I think, there has to be some gathering of data on what is good practice here, what works and what doesn't work, along with clarifying rules and regulations, because it is never going to be an either/or. It is going to be something in the middle. As a manager, it is time to address the variability within institutions. How they organize to approach this issue is a fundamental challenge in America. We are so pluralistic, and we have such different payer systems, so much complexity.

Dr. Bach: Dr. Clanton, how different is what you have just suggested compared to just more articulate guidance, for example? You are saying to certify things as opposed to creating templates.

Dr. Clanton: First of all, I am not really suggesting certification, but I was curious as to whether we could take the variability in implementation out of the system by giving a clean bill of health, by saying that if you do these things in general, this is the minimum amount of systematic implementation you need, and you may not need to do a lot of other things. So, I think if everybody knew what they were supposed to do and interpreted with precision what is written, we would take a lot of variability out of the system. The problem is that institutions have behaviors just as do individuals, and the institutional behavior in the face of uncertainty results in variable implementation. One systematic way of dealing with that is by creating a seal of acceptability or approval that allows you to say we don't have to do these five things if we do these six things. So, that was the only point I was making.

Dr. Bach: So an alternative is to pull the process out of the institutions and decentralize?

Dr. Clanton: Yes, right.

Dr. Moses: Our next presentation is by Joanne Pollak from Johns Hopkins talking about academic health center research impacts of the privacy rule.

Joanne Pollak, Esq., General Counsel and Vice President, Johns Hopkins Health System, Academic Health Center Research Impacts of the Privacy Rule: Thank you very much for giving me this opportunity, together with the others. I really feel the quality of the discussion here this morning is very, very high, and I think you are hearing both sides of the issue. In a minute, I will go into the four issues that I had planned to talk about today, but because some have already been covered to some extent, I don't want to spend as much time on them as anticipated. First, therefore, based on listening to some of your questions and the responses, I would like to make some preliminary remarks.

We all know that Dr. Zerhouni has a major initiative to promote collaborative research among different institutions; it is a very high priority for the NIH. Unfortunately, some of the unintended consequences of HIPAA discourage that very thing. I will relate, as Roberta did, some stories that emphasize that point. A researcher can be a provider, and thus a covered entity, or can be a researcher that is not, or is not part of, a covered entity. Mark Barnes, who will talk this afternoon, is the master of splitting into parts, and in the hybrid entity concept, you can actually have a hybrid person.

It has gotten to be so dysfunctional in terms of collaboration that if you are in the school of medicine at Hopkins, for example, and your research study is reviewed and approved and you are gathering protected health information from and through the covered entity, your research study is going to be part of a covered activity. If you are in the school of public health—which, although it was once within the covered entity, has now moved out—and you are a school of public health person, then you as a researcher, if you need information from the school of medicine, can go over to get it, but there are a lot of rules that apply to when the school of medicine can give it to you and what strings are attached. But if you somehow got that information and brought it into the school of public health, you don't have the difficult things applying to you, such as the accounting regulations that would apply in a covered entity.

As Marcy mentioned: what is the benefit of some of these privacy provisions, and what is the burden? If we find we have built in these impediments to collaboration and the sharing of information, then maybe we should step back and see what we really need to do to protect information that comes to us via a research study. What are the core important things? It shouldn't matter whether you are in the covered entity or outside the covered entity when you get your information from the covered entity. Both should be honoring what we say we do with the information. Let's decide on what that core is and do that.

Secondly, we have detailed authorization forms and informed consent forms, and we go to great lengths to tell participants what we are going to do with their protected health information. We put costly, very labor intensive systems in place for that. Then we turn the study over to the sponsor, and the sponsor has none of those limitations. When HIPAA came in, we were particularly concerned whether subjects were being greeted by elaborate consent forms describing how we will protect their information, and then there was the language at the bottom notifying them that once the information goes to an uncovered entity, we can't assure privacy law protection. What does that mean to a research subject? They trust Johns Hopkins. They trust your institution. They don't expect us to give away their information to outsiders who may do everything that we told them we were not going to do with their information.

I would say that, depending on the year, I spend about 20 percent of my time negotiating some very core restrictions with sponsors on the data that they get from us, because so often it is identifiable, and it is not enough to be a limited data set. We just ask for a few core things: that they not market with our data; they not call up the person and talk about enrolling in another study started by the sponsor; that they not share it with others.

If we are going to look at the Privacy Rule again, we need to think about a way to not just leave it to covered entities—I know there are jurisdictional issues and so forth—but I think there are ways, if it were in the regulations or in whatever it takes to be certified, that when you hand things off, people have to agree to certain things. If only one institution is doing this, it is very hard because the next institution doesn't do it, and the sponsor says I will take my study somewhere else. Why should I be bothered with all your restrictions? So, it is that uniformity again.

I need to mention something in connection with treatment, payment, and health care operations that was mentioned at the beginning of the day. Research was not seen as part of the core business that HIPAA was covering, and yet research is the core of our mission in many respects. Trying to differentiate between what is deemed to be part of our mission and for which we can use protected health information and what we need permission for is a difficult crosswalk.

I will just summarize the first of the issues I planned to discuss, because we talked a little bit about it already. There are, as you know, two different forms, informed consent and authorization. They can be combined, and that does not pose a problem. However, particularly in multi-center trials, some institutions allow a non-IRB to approve these authorization forms, and they are not consistent with what one would expect to see under the human research protection rules. If you are enrolling in a clinical trial you would expect your information to be used in that clinical trial, and whatever the rules are with respect to the use of that information would have to be consistent, and yet there are some very arcane differences that lawyers will tell you about. Well, it is better to use this form and that form, and it is better if you do this to give yourself more flexibility.

It shouldn't be that difficult. If we are talking about transparency—here is your information; here is how we are going to use it; here is who is going to receive it from us. That should be the same for an Office of Human Research Protections (OHRP) study, an FDA study, or under HIPAA. How are we going to deal with it in terms of regulations? One thought before was—and it is also in the SACHRP recommendations—to look to the Common Rule. If you meet those basic things that we think are important under the Common Rule, that should be enough, although I agree that since it only covers federally funded research, non-federally funded research needs to be added. I think that if we could harmonize so that the IRB/Common Rule provides the single oversight, people would not be confused by being confronted with two different forms resulting in lower accruals into trials. I think amending the HIPAA privacy regulations to allow use of personal information in research if the Common Rule or FDA rules are met is the solution. If those federal rules are not met, then the HIPAA privacy regulations would apply

The next item is authorization for future unspecified research. I do not believe this would require a regulatory change. This has really been an interpretation. Just as OCR noted that the agency felt passionate about privacy, I think the people who have spoken about research here today feel passionate. This is a real problem. We need to decide how we can be passionate toward a common goal, those core things that we want to protect for people. It seems to me that research subjects should be allowed to give tissue with the understanding and permission that it can be used for the next hundred years, as long as certain parameters are observed. Whoever uses the tissue for research should agree on the same core issues and protections that were defined for the initial research. I think it is very, very confusing to people, particularly in our cancer research studies, to be confronted two years after the original trial with another authorization form when they are not enrolling in any new research or new clinical trial. I think the Common Rule, FDA rules, and the interpretation of the HIPAA privacy regulations should be the same, that is, a person may consent to future unspecified research if the description of what is allowed is sufficiently clear, and I believe that this change does not require an amendment to the HIPAA privacy regulations; instead a change in HHS's interpretation of the Privacy Rule would be needed.

Accounting for disclosures in research has been alluded to. I think that everyone agrees that this has been a very difficult issue, and many of us have been saying that it really doesn't provide additional privacy protection. For example, if a record study gets approved under a waiver (which would trigger the accounting requirement), the information has already been looked at by the time the person gets the accounting. Does it help that person to get an accounting of the 600 retrospective studies that were done at Hopkins that might have used their information? Or do they want to know that any physician or practitioner who is allowed to do record research at that institution is going to protect those core values of not sharing with non-researchers, of protecting identifiability in publication, for example, in use of that information?

There are two ways people in research have reacted to the accounting requirement. They do the accounting, although it is found very difficult and very annoying. Or the requirement is ignored. From a regulatory point of view, when we are saying to our researchers you must comply with all of these OHRP rules, you must comply with all these FDA rules, and then they come to the HIPAA rules, and there is some variability in whether people say they are going to do it: some just don't do it. That is not a good compliance posture for any institution. Rules should be important, should be meaningful, and should be obeyed. Some rules are seen as not important and not helpful to people, and, therefore, there is a feeling that there is not a need to comply with some of them. Accounting, in particular, is one of those, because it is not a core value, at least to most researchers. They feel passionate about that in the same way that privacy groups feel passionate on the other side. I believe the solution is to amend the HIPAA Privacy regulations to state that if the Common Rule or FDA rules are followed, no accounting for disclosures would be required. If the Common Rule or FDA rules are not followed, then an accounting would be required.

This last issue, HIPAA Privacy Rule coverage of medical archives, is really just sort of a footnote that may be relevant to some institutions, where you actually move medical records over to archives. We have medical archives at Hopkins, and there are all sorts of materials in them. Because of the definition of protected health information (it either originated in, was maintained by, you received it, you actually created it), a lot of these historical letters and records are full of protected health information. It is not a problem generally for clinical and record research by our own usual medical researchers. The problem is that archives are used by lots of people who are not the kind of researchers that you ordinarily would think of, the press, the kind of persons who are doing a study on a famous individual, and so forth.

Because we believe that the words mean what they say, this requires that the archivists go through and redact the protected health information from the letters and other materials. Sometimes it is just somebody having a cold or something very minor, and you say to yourself that probably wasn't what was intended here. What was intended is that a covered entity cannot evade the Privacy Rule by archiving medical records. So, we need a dialogue about how we can resolve this problem. It's burdensome and the application of the minimum necessary standard is uncertain. HIPAA privacy regulations should apply only to true medical records, not all protected health information maintained in the archives.

Secondly, there is no vehicle for very old protected health information when you can't find anybody to give you consent to publish identifiable information. It is unclear whether a state, or even a federal, court has the authority to say that you can actually publish protected health information, because the regulations say that you must have an authorization. There is no waiver for publication. For example, you have someone who lived in the 1860s during the Civil War. It's very interesting historically, but can you publish it? It is the in medical archive, but you can't find a relative for the decedent. Do you say, I don't think there will be a complaint, and you take the business risk? The HIPAA privacy regulations need to provide a vehicle for publication of protected health information when no one is available to provide an authorization, perhaps a privacy board or a court.

There are a lot of medical archivists, who are concerned about the reach of HIPAA. One solution proposed was to move the medical archives outside the covered entity. Well, we can't do that. We have the protected health information, and there are rules for handing it out to anybody, so you can't "disinfect" it. Another solution might be to give the information, not to the medical archives, but to somebody else that is a non-covered part of the entity, and we wouldn't have the problem, but, that doesn't make sense. In other words, there are certain core things we should be doing for privacy to protect people. We shouldn't be playing games. Because of the dichotomy between covered and non-covered, we are seeing foreign repositories of tissue and other information because of HIPAA which is disadvantaging American universities and American researchers. I don't think you should split a researcher so you can say now you are protecting people's privacy and now you don't have to protect their privacy. Again, that doesn't seem to make sense; we should be coming back to the core of what we need to do.

These solutions are not easy. However, now that we are three of four years into it, we can sit down and have a dialogue. I am not sure there was receptivity at the beginning. There wasn't an understanding on the institutions' part of how passionate the feeling was at DHHS and then OCR, but also I don't think there was a full understanding at OCR of the complexity and the problems that are being created because of something that was intended to do good but is getting in the way of the flow of information needed for research purposes. So, those are just a few things, and I would welcome any questions.

Dr. Moses: Thank you for your presentation, and thank you for staying on time. Do we have questions or comments? Shall we go on to Donna Boswell, talking about impact on pharmaceutical company research?

Donna Boswell, Esq., Partner, Hogan and Hartson, Washington, DC, Privacy Rule Impact on Pharmaceutical Company Research: I am a health care lawyer at Hogan and Hartson, and I was helping our clients with HIPAA-like issues before there was HIPAA. I want to speak today about the impact of HIPAA on the programmatic research of sponsoring companies. I was pleased to be asked to come on behalf of Pharmaceutical Research and Manufacturers of America (PhRMA), but we also represent biotechnology companies and academic medical centers, as well as medical device companies. So, many of the stories I am going to tell you will also come from my experience in dealing with other than PhRMA members.

Pharmaceutical companies' and medical device companies' programmatic research is separate from their marketing departments. You should be aware that the people who conduct clinical research and who are the custodians of the research data sets at research companies do not talk to the marketing arm. Almost every company that I know that is big enough has research buildings with absolutely no computer access to any of the research databases by anybody in marketing or anybody with oversight by marketing. In setting up compliance protocols on the research side of the house, it is really key that nobody with any level of supervision over the marketing side or even recruiting has access to research databases.

For the most part, the research databases are obtained with the informed consent of the participants, and companies are extremely indebted to the beneficence of human beings who volunteer to be enrolled in these sometimes risky trials. They are very grateful for IRBs at academic medical centers and others that look out for and help understand and think through the risks and how to provide appropriate informed consent. That said, they are research companies, and they regard the data that they collect as really, really important.

The scope of the permission to use those data is something that they will argue is a serious matter, because anything that severely limits use of data for which millions of dollars have been spent is just not acceptable. They are not opposed to getting permission from the individual, not at all. But anything that looks like an artificial impediment to their ability to get permission to use that subject's data, whether it is from a repository under the repository rules or whether it is just a data set that needs to be reanalyzed once they get a little further along in their program, is really problematic for their important programmatic research.

That is why, when I think about HIPAA and research, sometimes I think we are talking about HIPAA versus research. From the company's point of view, since HIPAA doesn't apply to them, it is not something that they are involved in. It is both a possible relief, but also a possible problem because now everybody thinks that they are going to be careless with the data. Since the Privacy Rule doesn't apply in non-covered entities, the presumption is that the research data are unprotected. You heard it this morning. We talked about researchers who are "outside" who don't have restrictions on what they do with the data. But in truth, from a programmatic research point of view, those data are locked down because no company wants a competitor to find out anything about them. So, the data are very much protected.

So, what is the impact? First, I want to make the point that other people have made. With respect to research, there is no evidence that HIPAA has improved the protection of privacy of individuals. We do have evidence of increased confusion on the part of study participants. There are all kinds of reports back from the proctors and the monitors that there is confusion about the multiple forms and about some of the required statements that are in the forms. Our experience has been similar, that IRBs are hesitant to waive some of those required statements that don't make sense.

You have heard about the variability. Coordinating multi-site trials is a huge problem because of the differences in HIPAA interpretations in and among trials. We are seeing some evidence that there are site selection differences, based on the complexity of HIPAA negotiations. It was mentioned that smaller hospitals can't fully understand and get comfortable with things. They are having a much harder time, and so some of the principal investigators that you might want to involve in a multi-site trial might have a much harder time convincing their institutions to participate.

We also see in programmatic research for our companies that some epidemiologic approaches and analyses are affected, as Dr. Ness has said, because you just can't get complete enough data. There have been some reports of difficulty in following up on anomalies in clinical research, and I will talk a little bit more about that. There is definitely increased administrative cost that is built into the financing for a trial. Unfortunately, the biggest effect, I think, is that it has created an adversarial climate. I think we are seeing much more of an us versus them approach in the research situation than was the case previously, and not because of increased infractions, but just a general suspicion about what is or might be going on and a lack of understanding about what data protections are already available.

From my point of view, the roots of the problem lie in the lack of clear jurisdiction for putting this all together. There are competing purposes that are served by the two different schemes in the Common and Privacy Rules, and, in spite of the plea for harmonization, I am not sure we have discovered a basis to work toward harmonization. The objective of HIPAA is excellent: protecting privacy while ensuring health care and health benefits by keeping protected health information within covered entities. On the research side, however, research institutions are trying to both protect research and the privacy of those who choose to participate in research. The Privacy Rule starts with an absolute prohibition on the access to and use of protected health information in research unless you meet certain threshold conditions. There is not the kind of presumption that research in and of itself is a good and necessary activity, something that people might well want their data used for. Certainly, with respect to the smaller institutions, there is a big problem finding people with enough sophistication to deal with the very complex and voluminous guidance on HIPAA rules for research.

These are problems for covered entities. They affect sponsors trying to get access to data only indirectly. Sponsors have to go where they can get the data that will enable their programmatic research. If it is not going to be academic medical centers or the kinds of databases that we have created before, it will be elsewhere. We will not be shutting down research just because of the complexities and costs of particular centers.

Everybody knows about the overlapping jurisdiction of the OHRP and the FDA guidances. We have been comfortable with them. Although they prescribe different rules, we have a pretty clear understanding of when and how we get those together. We know how to do it. IRBs understand it, and they tell us how to do it on the sponsor's side, and we comply. It is not a problem at all.

HIPAA is an entirely different authority. It overlaps both OHRP and FDA rules. Although there has been some helpful guidance, the effect of

HIPAA is not uniform. It doesn't affect all the research. It only affects some aspects of research and research by some people. You have heard this mentioned already, this definition of who the covered entity is versus who the university is, who the research community is.

The impact of this slippery hybrid definition is that, as a sponsor or as a legal advisor to a sponsor, I need to be quite clear who I am contracting with when I go to research oversight. If both Pittsburgh and Hopkins have different parts of their institutions that are covered by HIPAA, I need to be very clear about that and about their HIPAA relationships in contracting to pay for my clinical research, for services to analyze data for a multi-site or a multi-national trial. Because the DHHS/OCR chose to add new specifications that apply when a covered entity engages in research and prohibited all disclosures other than in accord with new procedures that it articulated, the approach to protecting privacy taken by the HIPAA regulations is intended to be a regulatory hurdle between researchers and data generated in the ordinary settings in which clinical care occurs. That is a real problem. Research facilities that are not covered entities have a regulatory advantage over those that are subject to HIPAA. We have guidance for the various rules, but I am not sure we have anybody that has the jurisdiction to get the guidances harmonized, to advise on how to put the HIPAA parts together with the FDA and Common Rule parts, and as a lawyer I am going to be interested to see as we go forward whether we can find somebody that can do that.

I want to get to some of my details. I am concerned about the lack of transparency in the regulations. All of the guidance that we pour over in trying to figure out how to do research in spite of the complexity, goes to creating a lack of transparency. I think lack of transparency hurts people that want to participate in research or to ensure that their data or their biological materials are available for research. I think it also hurts researchers who get careless about what it means to comply. I think we need clear rules in order to make sure that people understand what is going on.

If I want to contract for data research, and I have an epidemiologist who wants to do data research and wants to put together multiple databases, the data research is subject to different compliance obligations based on who holds the data: a covered entity, a business associate of a covered entity, a data repository under NIH jurisdiction, a clinical research organization, a data recipient under obligations imposed by a form signed by the data subject. A researcher doing retrospective research needs both a data pedigree of each of these databases and a lawyer to help determine what must be done to assure that the privacy interests of data subjects are being protected in accord with law, to make sure of HIPAA compliant access to those data. That is not the way we need research to be done. We need some understanding of best data practices in an epidemiological research context or in an outcomes research design that applies to everybody who is doing research. We don't need everybody to be just making inquiries about who did you get your data from.

I think we also have a risk problem as a result of the complexity. The complexity and risk is all on the covered entities. Different institutions will have different appetites for risk, and faced with complexity, many of them just refuse to get involved. HIPAA is a very risky sort of statute, in spite of the fact that there have not yet been civil penalties imposed. There might well be any day now, and institutions that are risk averse, institutions whose structure doesn't provide for a lot of lawyer time to do careful assessments of risk, are just not going to be able to manage, for example, assessing what might constitute the minimum necessary information.

Early on, many of the sponsor companies attempted to understand HIPAA and provide guidance to IRBs and to academic medical institutions and others who didn't have professional staff time. Unfortunately, that didn't work because those with the expertise are the ones who want the data. So, this adversarial relationship that we have set up, as Mr. Holden said earlier, doesn't create the kind of trust environment for collaborating or for sharing expertise. I think this is a shame because it is very difficult to provide consulting services if you are a research sponsor company or even if you are a data management company when the penalty for your error is borne by someone else.

We are seeing some risk avoiding or self-protective kinds of behavior. I had great hopes for the data use agreement. There are some problems with the limited data set definition, of course. If you are a medical device company, you can't use the limited data set because device serial number is not acceptable in a limited data set. But we have a problem with the limited data set also, because who can sign the data use agreement? The risk is on the covered entity. If the IRB determines a waiver is unnecessary, and I should get a limited data set, then who signs that agreement on behalf of the covered entity that says they understand that the sponsor that gets this limited data set will manage it according to the perceived risk and obligation to police how that limited data set gets used. Whether that person is a trustworthy person, creates a level of risk. If I am dealing with a big academic medical center with compliance programs set up, I will be in good shape for finding somebody who can sign, but if I am dealing with somebody who has a really unique patient population and who is willing to do it, but that doctor isn't able to get somebody at the institution to deal with the risk and sign, again, my research is not going forward.

I want to skip ahead to the hybrid entity. It is in the guidance, and it works. Once lawfully disclosed to a researcher under HIPAA, the use and further disclosure of data are no longer subject to HIPAA, which means that you can sort of carve up your institution and have hybrid people who shift from one side to the other depending on what role they are playing. But in the research context this feels slimy, and people don't like it. It makes people very anxious as they go from one side to another. I am not sure I would know which hat I had to put on. It is not the right answer, and it is not the kind of a culture that we have in our IRB communities regarding what it means to protect patients from research risk. We have got to get harmonization back to where it is not just a sneaky lawyer trick.

You have heard about authorization and consent. It is also a problem for the sponsors when IRBs think that in reconciling the differences between them, they have to impose on the sponsor/recipient the same use restrictions that would apply if the sponsor was a covered entity. This goes well beyond the kind of restriction that Joanne talked about, such as promises not to use the data in marketing. The real problem arises when a sponsor can't use data for anything other than one specific protocol. As I said earlier, that is unacceptable. So, I end up spending time negotiating with lawyers or privacy officers, who are advising IRBs on the informed consent language once the HIPAA required statements get into it.

Our big problem with respect to this is that the required HIPAA statements together with historical broad consent for research uses upon admission are really a recipe for disaster, both from the HIPAA prohibition on future uses of data, as well as the notice that once the research company gets your data, it is not protected by HIPAA. Well, no, it is not protected by HIPAA but it is protected by a variety of other things. Nevertheless, the IRBs exhibit some real lack of understanding of what this reconciliation can mean and the waiver authority that they have.

I am going to share my stories, too, examples typically from smaller IRBs and their privacy officers of things that we have encountered. Some IRBs, or more usually the privacy officer advising the IRB, think that HIPAA requires inclusion in the informed consent of a prohibition, once the data are transferred, on the sponsor using the research for anything other than the particular specified research protocol. I can't have sponsored research with a site that insists on that kind of prohibition, because it is a waste of my money. They don't have to say, you can do anything you want, but I can't have the prohibition.

Some IRBs think HIPAA requires them to prohibit in the informed consent any statements about how the sponsor will use the data. So, some IRBs say you can't say this is how you are going to protect the data, or you are going to use it for cancer research, or you are going to make it available for cancer research under oversight of some other IRB, because that is not under IRB supervision. If I get that kind of a prohibition, I am perhaps wasting my money doing a study at that site.

In my worst example, the privacy officer who was advising the IRB said you can't have any of these statements in the informed consent, and what do you wish to do anyway. You should just go use the data any way you want because HIPAA says you can, and that is the required result. Well, that is just not true. Before HIPAA, the bulk of our practice in the privacy space was in advising companies that sponsor research on how to dot every "i" and cross every "t" to ensure that they had valid consent and permission for every data point submitted to FDA. Everything had to be obtained with valid patient consent or a waiver of consent. There are many restrictions that apply to sponsoring companies. I can't be just saying, fine, I will just go use the data, even though the forms say that I can't use the data. I will never be able to use those data at the FDA.

We have had some physicians and staff, usually staff participating in clinical trials at academic medical centers, who think, once a person is no longer in a trial, that they can't report adverse events, or anomalies, or things that might need follow-up by the company. This is really dangerous. Once a person withdraws, we have to protect her or his privacy and ensure we are not collecting data, given the absence of consent. But when there is an anomaly that occurs that might be related to the use of the investigational article, we have got to make sure that it gets into proper reporting chan-nels. It has been rare, but it happens occasionally, and increasingly the staff at sponsored companies find it necessary to spend some time counseling privacy officers at, again, usually less sophisticated institutions on why it is critical that their medical staff report the information notwithstanding the fact that the patient withdrew consent.

That is my biggest set of worries. Obviously, our concern is with future unspecified research and our ability to obtain patient consent for that. We are also among those who are very anxious about the impact on science of the selection bias in epidemiological studies mentioned by Dr. Ness.

Dr. Moses: I have sort of a broad question. It seems to me that if we are going to take a serious look at this and try to correct some of the problems, we need evidence, data, on the impact. I think AHRQ does have some data, and that is the reason we are having Ms. Stocks reporting later. But the question is, how can we design a study to get the data, to be able to show the negative or positive impact of the Privacy Rule? Roberta, I don't know whether you would be the best to answer as an epidemiologist or do any of you have thoughts on this?

Dr. Ness: My sense is that the best you are going to be able to come up with is survey data. My concern about surveys that have been done to date is that there is a huge selection bias in who is responding. So, I think that there would have to be a tremendous effort put forward to capture the entire universe of individuals who are conducting clinical research of various types. Moreover, I would say that a parallel survey should be done of the participants or the potential participants in research studies, because one of the very important questions that has been raised is whether HIPAA and the Privacy Rule are having any positive impacts. So I think we have to hear from both sides of that equation.

Dr. Betty Ferrell, Research Scientist, City of Hope National Medical Center: I have a slight disconnect from this morning. I work in an NCI designated cancer center, and I have been there for 17 years and have been on the IRB for the last 15 years. Probably one of every three hours at IRB meetings is taken up by HIPAA regarding what protocol can't be approved, what protocol is denied, what protocol has been in the works for 12 months, what trial has not been able to accrue, and so on. So, I am not sure why we are not capturing that this is a really urgent issue that is so important from a cancer center perspective.

On the question that you just posed of where are the data—one of the problems in capturing this issue is the variance institution by institution as to what research they are trying to conduct. Often, the epidemiologic studies are investigator initiated studies. My institution for example is trying to do a lot of work in pediatric cancer survivorship where we propose follow up studies for which the protocols are denied because of the problems we have been talking about.

I think that one way would be to do some case analyses in selected cancer centers, for example, to actually gather data on the protocols that were considered in that institution over the last six months, group clinical trials, epidemiologic studies—what was the impact? How many protocols were never opened? How many were opened but could never accrue? And that would give a more direct picture?

Dr. Bach: Setting aside the good aspects, which I think are implicit, but also need better documentation, I am trying to listen to this taking some of my own experience into account, to determine to what extent all the scary things in these presentations are due to bad implementation, miscommunication, poor comprehension, that is, user problems, and how much is bad regulatory structure. To the extent it is the latter, how much of that can be solved by guidances versus rulemaking versus legislation?

Ms. Pollak: Of the suggestions that I made, three out of the four required a regulatory change. One, in my view, could be done by clarification, such as permission for future unanticipated research; I think it is an interpretation of the words in the Rule. But the whole context of what are we trying to do to protect participants may require stepping back and examining how implementation should be organized. Should an additional requirement for the core values we've discussed be assigned to IRBs with expansion of their jurisdiction to non-federally funded studies for privacy issues, or should we work with the regulations as they are which would mean some amendments. I do think regulatory change will be needed in any event.

Dr. Moses: I have a question just to follow-up on the point I brought up before. How can PhRMA participate in this? Maybe Donna or David Parkinson could answer. Would PhRMA be willing to fund studies, or do they have their own data?

Dr. Parkinson: I suspect they would fund the studies, but they would probably be considered a conflicted party in terms of doing the studies.

Dr. Moses: Are there PhRMA data on what this is costing?

Ms. Boswell: I doubt it because what generally happens is that it is some poor staff person who just gets consumed by doing HIPAA negotiations. It would just be additional man hours. So, I doubt there are data that would assign a specified amount of time spent on HIPAA compliance as is being suggested about the IRB protocols. I think the IRBs are a much better data source, because there you will have a record. I will just have a record that I have got more people on staff at some company.

Dr. Parkinson: We could probably come up with documentation of increased costs, you know, delays, cancellations, transfer of work out of the United States, et cetera, et cetera. But nobody is going to be sympathetic to that. The real issue is what is happening with knowledge creation. I describe myself to be on the spend side of the company. My job is to understand how to treat cancer and to develop tools to that end. To the extent that the ability to achieve that mission is affected, then I think society is paying a price and needs to balance it with the potential gains.

While I can appreciate the benefits outside of the world of clinical research, which I understand from listening this morning that HIPAA was created for, I have much less understanding even after all this conversation as to what benefit this process has brought to the world of clinical research as opposed to the impediments. Certification might be one solution, but overall I'm not sure of the relevance of HIPAA to clinical research. I am still unclear about what was not protected before that is being protected now.

Dr. Ness: I would just like to clarify that a case-based approach to surveying IRBs is an outstanding idea, although I emphasize that should be complementary to surveying the researchers and participants. I say that because reporting from IRBs is not going to capture, for instance, the additional costs, the additional time, the sites that were approached but weren't able to participate. I am very much hoping that the IOM will do a study. I would see that there would be intentionally multiple approaches used which in concert would give you a picture of what is going on.

Ms. Wilder: I think the framing of the question as what is being protected now that wasn't being protected before is a good idea, although I think we don't know the answer. My guess is we could and should come up with an answer to that and also to Peter's question about how much of this just requires more education. Perhaps much of it requires more education, but the fact that it has been so hard for so many smart people to figure out how to manage under the Privacy Rule tells me two things.

First, your question will be answered when we start talking about harmonization. Was it being done before and is this adding anything? Second is simplification. If, we haven't figured out how to handle the Rule, and it still continues to be so complicated, maybe if we harmonize and simplify, privacy might not need to be this hard. It is going to be an effort to create what are best practices then. What are the principles, and how do you make it simple?

Dr. Patricia Ganz, Professor of Medicine, UCLA: One of the things that was addressed earlier on is that many of these issues are in the Common Rule already, and there was already a lot of variability in the way in which IRBs were handling their work. I happen to be at UCLA where our IRB was of the most restrictive in the nation, and we had all of these things in terms of researcher contact and all of the privacy issues already imbedded in our IRB process, which took six months to get through anyway.

In fact, therefore, HIPAA didn't change us too much, because we just had another consent form change adding HIPAA authorization, but in terms of the IRB principles and research principles, they didn't change. I suspect that HIPAA did change sensitivity of many IRBs to enforcing the privacy elements within the Common Rule, and maybe that is where the impact has occurred. Perhaps there is higher compliance with those elements as a result, but it came about in a very arcane way given that, as was said, the Privacy Rule was not meant to emphasize research; it was really meant to focus on the covered entity and data transfer.

To me it caused a paradoxical improvement in use of the Common Rule, but at a huge administrative burden and cost. So, that is what I am taking away from this discussion.

Dr. Robinson: If there were 20,000 complaints about the way this process is being handled, the assumption might be that some of those are coming from IRBs, and if the Office for Human Research Protections has a vested interest in wanting to see that process run smoothly, HHS might want to be supportive of an activity that would look at this, not only from OCR's standpoint, but also from OHRP's perspective. The whole basis of the consent dispute goes back to consent being a process, rather than a document. To the degree that the department wants to go ahead and get to the bottom of this because of its investments in research, not just cancer, but all the different kinds of research, it might be helpful to engage those IRBs that have already gone on the record as identifying a problem to see to what degree it is fitting into one of these different patterns that we see.

Dr. Burish: Based on what I heard this morning, I think the problems that have been identified can be put into one of three categories, one of which would benefit from more research. First, there are some problems with the current HIPAA regulations where there is wide agreement that we need to find a way to fix them. There is not a controversy about whether change is needed; there is, rather, a challenge about how to make the changes. Second, there is a group of concerns about which there is a controversy. The controversy is about giving up some privacy protection for people versus advancing research needs. Those concerns could be productively addressed by collecting data which would help assess risk versus benefit. I will come back to that. The third category includes problems that are not primarily with the regulations themselves, but primarily with their implementation and so forth. You would want try to address the first two areas before addressing the third area, because some of the problems in the third area might disappear if you could resolve some of the concerns in the first two areas.

In terms of gathering data, while some questions may require comprehensive data about the application of HIPAA, other questions can be answered with more limited data. I doubt the general public cares greatly about how much time IRBs spend on HIPAA, because if they think the time is usefully spent, fine, spend whatever time is required. But there are two questions that have emerged about which I would guess the general public has great concerns. First, what science isn't being done that could cure cancer or cure AIDS, because HIPAA is slowing or stopping it? Second, what information is not reaching patients, such as information about treatment alternatives and trial opportunities, because HIPAA prohibits giving the information to patients?

Data on those two questions: what science isn't being done and what patients aren't getting that they might want, I think, could be gathered through case studies at four or five, or some group of, major medical centers. Anecdotes become data at some point. Maybe, the Forum or IOM could commission such studies from available funds, contracting the studies out with some company. This is more the sociology of collecting information about behavior, if you will. I do not think PhRMA should conduct these studies, but it would be very useful if we could see that they are conducted.

Dr. Moses: Well, except PhRMA might do something about the impact. I think moving research out of the U.S. is particularly important.

Dr. Parkinson: I doubt if you are going to get complete transparency and discussion of that topic. I am just telling you the way it is.

Mr. Holden: I would argue, though, that there are data that companies can provide about the impact of HIPAA on their research activities. It may be a very narrow set, but it would be relevant to the issue of complementary data to try to at least get some reality. There is too much research being funded through industry not to include it. So, the question is what are the qualifiers? PhRMA gathers all sorts of data for different purposes. There is no reason they can't do it here.

Dr. Burish: I agree. When I referred to PhRMA not being involved, I was talking about PhRMA not performing the studies, not about excluding them from providing any information.

Dr. Edward Benz, President, Dana Farber Cancer Institute: I want to add one other aspect to this that goes beyond stopping science or what science isn't being undertaken. It is whose science is going to end up changing the practice of medicine in this country. I offer this from the perspective of my part time job editing oncology for *The New England Journal of Medicine*. I and the editors in other specialty areas are increasingly seeing that the papers on discovery of relevant genomics and other advanced science are coming from the United States, but the applications are coming from Europe and Asia. Some of it, frankly, is because their health care systems are better organized, and their patient cohorts are easier to study.

But if the new change in medical practice from the use of pharmaco-genomic data, for example, comes from Scandinavia or from Korea, the comparison, importantly, of the new standard, leaving the ethnic factors aside for the moment, will be to an old standard of practice that isn't ours. You know, that is how studies are done. We increasingly have, as we read those papers, difficulty in understanding their applicability. I don't think the issue should just be framed in terms of competitiveness or just in terms of research that will or won't be done. It involves also this additional aspect, the origin of research that will affect our practice of medicine. That has got to be part of the equation because that is where our patients can really be affected. Is it going to be the kind of research that we can rationally apply to practice here?

Dr. Ferrell: I think, since our focus is cancer research, as the National Cancer Policy Forum, that the Forum might do a well constructed survey of cancer centers, stratified geographically and by type of center, to get some meaningful data about what's really happening at a cancer center level with researchers and protocols. Then PhRMA might perhaps do the same thing with their industry to present their data. Clearly we do need data if we are ever going to move forward.

Dr. Moses: Why don't we move on to the effect of the Privacy Rule on CDC and NCHS research and surveillance?

Dr. Ralph Coates, Associate Director for Science, Division of Cancer Prevention and Control, CDC and Dr. Catharine Burt, Chief Ambulatory Care Statistics Branch, Division of Health Care Statistics, NCHS, The Effect of the Privacy Rule on CDC and NCHS Research, Surveillance and Public Health Programs: *Dr. Coates:* I am going to talk about the effects of the privacy rule on research, which is what we have been talking about, but also add in the effects on public health practice, surveillance, and other types of public health programs. With regard to public health practice as opposed to research, the Privacy Rule expressly permits disclosures of HIPAA protected health information without individual authorization for the purposes of preventing and controlling disease, including but not limited to surveillance, investigation, and intervention by public health authorities authorized by law to collect or receive information.

The public health authorities to which this applies include CDC and other federal agencies, state and tribal health agencies, cancer registries, and their contractors by a grant of authority. With regard to public health research, there is no permission for disclosure of identifiable health information without individual authorization. So, public health research, including CDC's research, is governed by the same Privacy Rule and by the same other federal policies for protection of human subjects as any other federally funded research.

For example, on the public health surveillance side, the National Program of Cancer Registries (NPCR) was established in 1992 to develop population-based registries to collect diagnostic and treatment data on cancer in all 50 states and to help develop state laws requiring provider reporting of that information and protecting confidentiality. Other registry activities are similar to registry activities funded by NCI. There are now registries in all the states.

Between the passage of the HIPAA Privacy Rule and its implementation, there was a lot of confusion among the registries and providers, the covered entities, about the effects of HIPAA, the kind of confusion that has already been talked about with regard to research. The registries sought guidance from CDC, the North American Association of Central Cancer Registries (NAACCR), state legal departments, and many private firms on the new requirements and how best to communicate those requirements to the covered entities.

Guidance on the Privacy Rule was that it allows covered entities to disclose protected health information to registries as required by state laws. The registries may include both state public health agencies and their contractors, for example, universities. Providers are required to notify people whose information has been disclosed. HIPAA implementation involves substantial time and effort by most of the registries, and even then some problems in research continue. For example, certain entities, physician's offices, which are much less familiar with HIPAA regulations often don't understand the policies and how they work. The registries are questioned about some specific kinds of activities, for example, quality audits requiring patient medical record review by the registry staff. So, registry communication with covered entities is an ongoing and continuing activity that requires additional effort.

With regard to public health intervention programs, I will use the National Breast and Cervical Cancer Early Detection Program which provides breast and cervix cancer screening to low income uninsured women to illustrate. The primary activities of the program are screening, follow-up, and case management, among others. The program funds these activities in all 50 states and with several tribes and territories. An activity of the program that is not as well known as the actual supervision of screening services is that the program providers, the covered entities, report screening and diagnostic information, including personal identifiers, to the state and tribal programs for quality assurance. Those programs then report linkable but not protected quality assurance data to a CDC contractor to allow us to do quality assurance as well. For example, New York State identified unusual screening outcome rates at some facilities. A subsequent public health investigation, which is something that is also excluded from the Privacy Rule requirements, led to the closure of one facility and additional training required in another.

Because private information was obtained by the program, women who had been screened in those programs could be called back and provided adequate screening services. Those data allow CDC to monitor the outcomes of its program such as the number of people screened and the outcomes.

A determination that the program is not a covered entity but is, in fact, a public health program funding the provision of health care is one of the issues that has been actively worked through with regard to HIPAA. The program has also had to work through ongoing communications with covered entities to enable the continued submission of surveillance data, including identifiable information, by more than 21,000 practices. Other issues included the ability of CDC staff and contractors to conduct medical record audits to evaluate the quality of the surveillance.

With regard to public health research, the problems encountered by CDC are probably similar to those encountered in non-public health research. They include confusion, delays in approval and implementation of research studies, reductions in the numbers of studies and questionable restrictions of access to information, and uncertain response rates in population studies.

Dr. Burt: We run a family of provider based surveys that are authorized under the Public Health Service Act to collect information that produces public use files of medical record type information that people can use to study the frequencies, rates, and relationships among provider characteristics and patient and visit characteristics.

I am going to tell you a little bit about the survey, so you can see how it intersects with HIPAA, about some of the modifications we used, and the effects on cooperation. The National Ambulatory Medical Care Survey is an annual survey of office based physicians, excluding radiologists, anesthesiologists, and pathologists. It is a multi-staged sampling design. We sample different locations around the country, and the sampling frame uses the master files of the American Medical Association/American Osteopathic Association to get to the physicians. Now, the goal, after a brief interview with the physician, is an abstract by the physician or practice staff of information from records of about 30 patient encounters during a one week reporting period.

In the past, we were considered exempt from human research regulation. We were only collecting information that was already collected someplace. Nobody had to collect anything different for our survey. With the implementation of the HIPAA Privacy Rule, we had to make a myriad of modifications. This is true for all our family-based surveys, actually. So, we had to change the introductory letters that we mailed to enlist the physicians before the data collection agent went out for their interview. Because we couldn't assume that physicians would know about all of the intricacies of HIPAA as it relates to research, we thought we had to give them some questions and answers about how they could still cooperate with us.

This accounting documentation increased the burden on the physicians to cooperate with the survey, because now they had to put something in the medical record to document the disclosure of information. We needed a data use agreement because when the doctor or the staff themselves abstracted the medical record information, we only collected information that was available under the data use agreement; no individually identifiable information was collected. However, oftentimes the physicians or their staff didn't have time to do medical record abstraction, and they asked our data collection agent, the U.S. Census Bureau, to do the abstraction. When that happens, the Census Bureau field representative may see incidentally the patient's name, even though we don't collect it. Therefore, it is disclosed, and we had to get IRB approval, the data use agreement, and the accounting documentation, et cetera.

So, there was a lot of training required of our field staff on the intricacies of the HIPAA privacy rule, a lot more provider materials, the provider web site, and all kinds of information. Then we had to actually make modifications to what data we collected. So, we don't collect any directly identifiable data, name, social security number, medical record number, among others. We do collect some indirectly identifiable information however, such as date of visit, date of birth, and the zip code. But most of the data that we collect is de-identified.

What about the response rates for these particular items, the ones that were indirectly identifiable, and some that were de-identified, before and after HIPAA? We found that the response rates for the sensitive items, date of birth and zip code, increased after HIPAA so that it was on a par with the non-sensitive items that we were collecting. On the other hand, the overall physician response rate which in the past had been around 70 percent declined slightly (3–4 percent) when the privacy rule went into effect, and is continuing to decline. Can I blame this on HIPAA? Well, this is not an experimental study; it is an association, so who knows. We had done a lot though to try to get the response rate up, but it didn't stay up. It came down. We also have some anecdotal information from our field staff. The first two anecdotes I have are from 2004 after HIPAA had been in place for about a year. Staff reported that they were getting increasing road blocks; doctors would use any excuse not to participate in the survey, and HIPAA was just one more. Doctors were more aware of HIPAA, and believed that they would be breaking the law or betraying patient privacy. They didn't really know what the law was. Our staff did see that the IRB letter that we gave and the data use agreement were good tools and helped on multiple occasions.

Now, earlier this year, when queried again about the effects of HIPAA on data collection, we were getting increasing road blocks again; staff thought the publicity about the setting of penalties, the information on the enforcement rule, might be related to our new difficulties. Even though nobody has been fined, that doesn't eliminate anxiety. The worst thing was that our field representatives instead of talking to the doctor or the office staff, in many locations found themselves referred to the practice's lawyer. Discussions with lawyers increase the time it takes for the field representative to get the physician to cooperate, and that means increased costs. So, we think HIPAA added about 10 percent to the cost of the survey because of the extra time that field representatives had to spend convincing doctors.

So, in summary, we think that the careful planning that we did forestalled a lot of problems. We did not have to close our operations down. We worked very hard to prepare all the needed materials, which you can now review on our newly created survey participant web page, and to understand the Privacy Rule. I think I knew every detail in that law, better than the doctors did. As was noted earlier, it seems that the research people actually knew what the law said, and the physicians didn't.

We incurred an increased cost due to extra training of the field representatives; it added an extra half a day to the interviewer training time, which was only about a day and a half to two days to begin with, and then the extra training in the induction time. There was possibly a negative effect on response rate. Although I don't think I can blame it all on HIPAA, the Privacy Rule certainly seems to be having an effect. We are in the early stages of a survey of our non-respondents. Several years ago, long before HIPAA, we surveyed to find out the reasons for non-participation. Now we will repeat the survey, except we will add a little item among HIPAA to see if that percentage is a reasonable size or is it in fact very small.

We have improved reporting on the sensitive items, which is very good. But we still need to continue to monitor this over time because whatever adjustments were made in the early phase of Privacy Rule implementation didn't resolve all the problems. People are still learning about how to do all this. I should also mention, anecdotally, that our hospital response rates have come down. They were around 94 percent. Now they are around 88 percent, although we have not seen any bias in the response rate. It's not that there is more non-response among smaller hospitals. I think someone said something about smaller hospitals being less able or motivated to manage the Privacy Rule and participate in research. We haven't seen that. So, it appears not to be biasing the results of our survey. But it has effected also the time that it takes for induction in our hospital surveys as well.

Mr. Feldman: You referred to the need to engage in authorization with respect to identifiable information because it inadvertently would be available to the abstractors?

Dr. Burt: If our field staff did the abstraction, they might see the sampling sheet, the people who were sampled for the abstraction, or they might see the name on the medical records. Some doctors will cover it up. Others don't.

Mr. Feldman: And the field staff are your employees or contractors?

Dr. Burt: They are the U.S. Census Bureau. They have their own set of confidentiality provisions. We have been collecting under authority of keeping data confidential for years. This is nothing new. But now HIPAA put the onus on the provider end. They share in the responsibility for keeping data confidential now. Yes, this was an interpretation. I will tell you that other government agencies interpreted "incidental" differently, but CDC felt if a field representative were to see a patient's name, that it was not incidental and could not be ignored, that it was part of the basic protocol of the data collection.

Mr. Feldman: You made the point, thank you.

Dr. Dennis Deapen, Director Los Angeles Cancer Surveillance Program and Professor of Preventive Medicine, University of Southern California, Negative Impact of HIPAA on Population-Based Cancer Registry Research: A Brief Survey (presented in writing to the Forum as part of this workshop): The Health Insurance Portability and Accountability Act (HIPAA) of 1996 was written to facilitate continuation of health insurance coverage among American workers who change employers, specifically "to amend the Internal Revenue Code of 1986 to improve portability and continuity of health insurance coverage in the group and individual markets, to combat waste, fraud, and abuse in health insurance and health care delivery, to promote the use of medical savings accounts, to improve access to long-term care services and coverage, to simplify the administration of health insurance, and for other purposes."

The Act contains a Privacy Rule, an extensive set of policies and procedures intended to protect the privacy of health information in the use and disclosure of data covered by the Act. Questions have been asked about the Privacy Rule and possible interference of health-related research. One issue of interest is whether there has been HIPAA-related interference with research by and access of researchers to cancer registries and registry information.

To respond to this question, a brief survey was conducted of the membership of the North American Association of Central Cancer Registries (NAACCR). NAACCR has 71 members representing population-based state, regional and provincial cancer registries in Canada and the U.S. and its territories. The majority of population-based cancer registries are not HIPAA covered entities. With the approval of the NAACCR Board of Directors, the survey was conducted via the Internet May 19–31, 2006.

Fifty-five responses were received. Two registries submitted two replies; those responses were consolidated into one reply for each registry. Five responses were submitted by hospital-based registries and were excluded. One response was submitted by a Canadian registry and was excluded since HIPAA is a U.S. law. Thus, of 71 members, responses from 47 registries are included, a response rate of 66%.

Question 1 asked "Has HIPAA been cited as the reason for actions that have interfered with non-research operations of our cancer registry?" The responses are shown in Table 1.

TABLE 1 Responses to Question 1

Number	Percent	Response
15	32	No
31	66	Yes
1	2	Don't know

Question 2 asked "Has HIPAA been cited as the reason for actions that have interfered with registry-based research? (check all that apply)". The responses are shown in Table 2.

TABLE 2 Responses to Question 2

Number	Percent	Response
12	26	No
9	19	Yes, has stopped or prevented a research project
32	68	Yes, has delayed a research project or caused it to take longer
17	36	Yes, has possibly introduced bias into a research project, e.g., made data collection on some cases more difficult than others
5	11	Not applicable

Population-based cancer registries are relied upon to produce reliable cancer incidence data for public health surveillance and research. Two-thirds of the registries responding to this survey indicated that HIPAA has been cited as the reason for actions that interfered with basic surveillance. Understanding the nature, magnitude and impact of this problem will require further research.

Population-based cancer registries are used in many ways for research including descriptive analysis of routinely collected data, special studies requiring collection of additional data from medical records, record linkage studies, and direct patient contact studies. This research may be conducted by registry personnel as well as external researchers. Sixty-four percent of respondent registries reported that HIPAA has been cited as the reason for actions that have interfered with research. Often, this interference increased the cost or imposed delays. Of greater concern, many registries also report the introduction of possible bias or complete disruption of the research.

No information was requested on the number of research studies that were impacted. More information on the nature, magnitude and impact of this problem will require further research.

Among respondent population-based cancer registries, the majority report that HIPAA has been cited as the reason for interference with both basic surveillance and registry-based research. Additional research could reveal the frequency, magnitude, and impact of the interference. Thanks are due for this work to the NAACCR Board of Directors, Dawn Gwinn, Charlie Blackburn, Kessa Deapen, and the survey respondents.

Dr. Moses: Next, we are having a presentation by Sarah Carr on the NIH perspective, questions about the impact of the privacy rule on NIH supported research.

Sarah Carr, Senior Advisor, Office of Science Policy, NIH, NIH Perspective: Questions about the Impact of the Privacy Rule on NIH Supported Research: NIH is very pleased to be participating in this Forum session, and we welcome your exploration of the HIPAA privacy rule and its impact on health research. I am standing in today for Dr. Lana Skirboll, the Associate Director for Science Policy at NIH, who was very sorry she couldn't be here herself, given how important the question of HIPAA's impact on research is to NIH. My presentation will focus on some of the concerns we have about inconsistencies between the Privacy Rule and other regulations covering research, and then I will share with you some or our questions about the Rule's impact on NIH supported research. I hope I don't sound redundant because the questions we have are some that you all have as well.

You are well aware, probably better than any other group, that this is a transformational time for biological and life sciences. Technological developments in molecular biology and information technology are converging, providing unprecedented opportunities to translate scientific discoveries into knowledge and products that will take medicine and health to a new level of care, one designed and tailored to the individual.

IT systems are making it possible to collect, store, and analyze voluminous amounts of patient data, both phenotypic and genotypic. But to realize the full promise of these extraordinary scientific opportunities in promoting health and treating disease, researchers must have access to large data sets and must be able to share them and combine and compare them with other large data sets, and this kind of research can present special data protection challenges. Protecting the privacy of research participants and maintaining the confidentiality of their data, as we heard today, has always been paramount to researchers and a fundamental tenet of clinical research.

In addition to the ethical principles that animate this commitment to the protection of privacy in data, researchers know on a pragmatic level that trust is central to the willingness of patients to participate in research. Protecting the privacy of participants and the confidentiality of their data has been part of a larger and older system of human subjects protection, as you have also heard today and know well from your own work. Common Rule and FDA regulations have been in place for many years. These rules require that privacy risks be addressed along with other risks of research, and many practical strategies have been used under this system to protect privacy and data.

The system recognizes the importance of maintaining an appropriate balance between protecting individual privacy and the ability to carry out research for the common good. Balancing the twin values of privacy and research was certainly a guiding principle during the drafting of the HIPAA Privacy Rule. For a number of reasons, however, we have begun to question whether the Rule struck the right balance between these two important goods. As you have heard today and know well, too, the Privacy Rule is a complex regulation, and it is a regulation that covers many other activities besides research. Research is just one and, in some ways, a small part of the Rule.

When the Rule was first implemented, some of the problems that arose were not unexpected. Like any complex regulation, time was needed to study and understand the Rule and how it works and how it interacts with other regulations at the federal and state level. HHS worked very hard through the Office for Civil Rights to develop guidances and educational materials to help the covered entities understand the rule and how to comply with it. As Sue McAndrew said, OCR sought input from NIH in developing materials specific to the research community, and I think these efforts undoubtedly were helpful when the Rule first went into effect.

I will now review some of the harmonization issues we see. As we discussed today, research is regulated by the Common Rule, FDA regulations at times, as well as the HIPAA Privacy Rule. There are important differences between the Privacy Rule and the Common Rule—for example, the scope and applications of the Rules differ; and they define key terms in different ways—that can result in confusion and inconsistency in interpretation. For us, identifiability is an important example. Under the Common Rule, individually identifiable refers to information that would allow an investigator to readily ascertain the identity of an individual or readily associate the information with the individual. Under the Privacy Rule, identifiability is defined in very specific terms; for information to be considered de-identified it may not contain any one of 18 data elements, and also the information cannot alone or in combination with other information allow the patient to be identified.

There are also important differences in the requirements for future research use of protected health information. This was an issue that a number of other presenters talked about today, and it is a concern to NIH as well. The Common Rule has been interpreted by OHRP to permit informed consents that are broader than for a specific study, whereas the current interpretation of the Privacy Rule requires authorizations to be study specific. There are also content differences between consents and authorizations. Even though an informed consent must address the privacy risks to subjects, the Privacy Rule has additional very specific requirements regarding the content of an authorization and what information is to be disclosed. We are hearing from investigators that these additional requirements tend to result in long complex forms that compound an already complex informed consent process. Do the differences between the Common Rule and the Privacy Rule enhance privacy protections, or do the differences create confusion that makes compliance more difficult? Does the Rule fill a real oversight gap or are the Rule's requirements adding burdens without really enhancing protections, and are the requirements discouraging participation in research? These are some of the questions we at NIH have, and we know that you have them as well. We look forward to any work that IOM can do to help answer these questions.

We haven't carried out a comprehensive assessment of the impact of the Privacy Rule on research, but we have been hearing concerns from the research community. These reports suggest that the Rule can present challenges to ensuring representative study cohorts, affecting scientific validity and robustness of study designs. The authorization requirement, for example, eroded the completeness of data in one well-established NIH registry. Prior to the Privacy Rule, almost all patients agreed to enroll, and after the Rule refusals ranged from five to fifteen percent. It is important to point out, however, that we aren't certain that enrollment in this study dropped becasue of the Privacy Rule. There appears to be a connection, but we need to probe further to determine whether the Rule is really the cause. Without a more certain understanding of cause and effect it's probably unfair to point to the Rule as the cause of the decline in this case. This is the sort of work we hope to do more of and to see others do, to delve more deeply into these research recruitment problems.

The Rule's requirements also appear to be causing delays in study initiation and extending the length of some trials. In one case, a collaborative study with industry was delayed due to protracted negotiations concerning HIPAA compliance. We have also heard concerns that the Rule may be precluding research altogether, and this is a concern raised earlier today too. This concern is also quite difficult to verify; we don't know what's not being done, and that might be, as someone else suggested, the most worrisome issue. The Rule also appears to be having particular effects on certain types of research. We have heard that multisite collaborative studies, studies involving databases and repositories, epidemiological and surveillance research, medical records and repository research, as well as international collaborations seem to be facing particular challenges.

The harmonization issues and the concerns we've been hearing raise some key questions for us. Are the problems isolated cases, or are they representative of a broader problem affecting the clinical research enterprise as a whole? How widespread are the Rule's effects on research? What is causing the difficulties? Is there a continuing misunderstanding of the Rule? Are investigators and privacy boards and IRBs still over-interpreting the Rule, reading too much into it? Will additional guidance help? Or are there more fundamental problems at work, and if so, what can be done about them? Another question for us is whether the complexity of the Rule and differences from the Common Rule create inefficiencies and barriers without providing any additional privacy protection. Are these difficulties going to increase, particularly given how complex the research environment is becoming and how much more data are being collected and shared on a broad and often global scale?

NIH has recently launched a number of important initiatives in which the Privacy Rule may present significant challenges. Some of these initiatives are products of the NIH Roadmap, which, as Joanne Pollak referenced earlier, is Dr. Zerhouni's plan for optimizing scientific discovery for human health by stimulating, and promoting scientific collaboration. Some of the important initiatives underway include the Cancer Bioinformatics Grid (CaBIG), the National Biospecimen Network, the Genetic Association Information Network (GAIN), the Genes and Environment Initiative (GEI), and the National Electronic Clinical Trials and Research (NECTAR) Network. All of these studies and initiatives involve collaborative research with multiple sites relying on access to specimens and associated data that will be collected and held over many years. Insuring highly representative samples and minimizing bias will be critical to the success of these projects and to the broad applicability of their findings. If the problems with the Privacy Rule persist, will these high priority research projects, which hold such promise for addressing our most pressing public health problems, be able to achieve their goals?

The research community, the patient community, and the public to a large degree are of one mind about the importance of research and the need for a supportive environment for research. Most of us want to see progress in the development of new diagnostic, treatment, and prevention approaches. We want the privacy of people who volunteer to participate in research and the confidentiality of their data to be protected. We want to see research efforts come to fruition and lead to advances in public health and the quality of life. The questions we posed today in this Forum about the Rule's impact on research need to be addressed in a systematic way and through discussions with the public, the patients, and the privacy advocates. Are there ways to reduce the complexity and burden of the Privacy Rule on research while continuing to provide the necessary privacy protections for research participants? NIH also thinks we need to share perspectives about the benefits of research and the value of privacy and collectively address whether these two important goals are still in balance. NIH would welcome and applaud such efforts.

Dr. Moses: Thank you Sarah. Questions or comments?

Dr. Ferrell: I think that this is a valuable opportunity to gather data. A survey of currently funded NIH extramural projects could give us this information. Especially since NIH funds such a variety of research, and a survey would include timely current projects. Specific questions could be asked regarding whether any of the problems we've talked about today have occurred. What are the benefits that have been derived? I think it could be done fairly promptly, and we would get a very good snapshot.

The second comment I want to make is that the impact of HIPAA is not just on the development of new agents. We have seen a huge impact on epidemiologic studies and on cancer control studies. We have a new RO1 funded in my institution, a follow-up of transplant patients and an evaluation of the impact on their quality of life and symptom management. HIPAA requirements with the consent form were creating such problems that the approval was delayed, and it required the intervention of the hospital counsel to alter the form to make accrual into this RO1 funded current study possible. So, I really think this is just a huge opportunity to get good information.

Ms. Carr: With regard to conducting a survey, you may know that there are certain requirements when an agency wants to survey more than nine people. So if NIH were to do this, it would actually take us a while to put it together and to get the appropriate permissions. Do you think it's important that such a survey be done by NIH? Would it make a difference if NIH did this kind of survey?

Dr. Moses: I think it would. If you, as a funding agency, are asking questions you are more likely to get a response.

Dr. Ferrell: I thought it was great this morning to see people involved in this important privacy issue. We want to work towards solutions, and I felt this morning's presentations were wonderful in proposing solutions we could try or that we have already tried. But our colleagues can't go forward and solve problems unless they are carefully and thoroughly identified. So, that is what this could do.

Dr. Moses: Let's go on to Paula Kim.

Paula Kim, Translating Research Across Communities (TRAC) Network and Mary Lou Smith, Y-Me, National Breast Cancer Organization and Co-Founder, Research Advocacy Network, Patient Advocacy Perspectives: Importance of Balancing Privacy Protections and Research Data Sharing in Advancing Public Health: *Ms. Kim:* I very much appreciate the opportunity with my colleagues at NIH to share a few minutes from the patient perspective. And I appreciated your comments this morning, Paul.

What I would like to do is not speak so much about the Rule itself, but about what is really important: all that you are working so hard to try to accomplish, balancing privacy with the research, so we can get to the bottom line—advancing public health. So, on the one hand, if we think about research, it cuts across ever part of the scientific spectrum. Our patients are very diverse also, they could be your family or friends; they are all patients nonetheless. And they are counting on all of us to provide them the hope that they need so that they can live well and survive their disease. If we think about everything that we have been trying to do here, and the discussion today has been terrific, in understanding the rules and the regulations, we are spending enormous sums printing literature to tell patients what their rights are. Part of what I heard this morning is maybe the Rule itself is not as bad as everybody might say, it is just the failure to interpret and failure to track and properly communicate. So, it could be that it all comes down to how we translate it, how we understand it, and who understands what. If we do a lousy job of it, then nobody understands that we have a problem. So, it is just a different language, and we need to learn to speak in the language of the people that we are trying to have understand because we are not our audience.

So, if we always keep that at the forefront, then I think we have got a half a shot at this. There are many dilemmas that patients face, dilemmas and decisions that they need to make, let alone have to worry about the formalities of paperwork. Let me give you an example, what is HIPPA? Now, that is not a new spelling. But I can tell you that there are numerous presentations given by people in agencies, researchers, whoever, where that is how it is spelled. What that says to me is well, okay, so maybe they are just parroting something. Maybe they never thought about what the acronym means, but I think it is an interesting question that if you were to say to the presenter who got it wrong, so, "HIPAA, what do those words mean," maybe they will stumble, maybe they won't. But, again, I think it speaks to my point.

But these are issues that patients deal with, and the question, "Am I going to live?", that is really the most paramount thing in their minds. "What is it going to take to survive?" I think Paul made a great point this morning, because he is a product of research in terms of his ability to be here. If it weren't for the research, he and many other people wouldn't be here. I think we need to keep that at the forefront, to not lose sight of the fact—yes, it is important to do all these other things—that however we balance the issues, we must preserve the ability to keep moving forward because if we stay still, if you are not advancing and you are treading water, you are, in effect, going backwards.

We are trying to balance privacy and research here, to advance public health. That is our goal. What I heard today is that we have federal law and we have state law and sometimes those two don't match up and that is one place where there is confusion. We have HIPAA law, IRBs and the Common Rule. I liked Donna's presentation in which she talked about the confusing sometimes overlapping and sometimes separate parts of the regulations. If it is that confusing to talk about, imagine when you are trying to understand it or to implement it and you get your hand slapped when you failed to implement according to somebody who says you blew it.

Then we have the letter of the law, but we also have common sense, and I think that is something that we need to figure out how to balance;

it's a tough one. But the patients look at things from the standpoint of benefit and risk, and I can tell you from my work in the pancreatic cancer community—and we all understand those difficulties—that patients will risk whatever it takes when they are looking at mortality. Are they being overprotected?

My dad was diagnosed and died in 75 days. He understood what risk was. We understood it. We understood the risks that we were willing to take and the things that we were willing to give up for a possible good outcome. Look at the HIPAA law and what it was attempting to do and the section that had this word about simplification in the authorization language. But, in fact, everybody keeps saying it complicated more than it simplified anything.

The misuse issue of information seems to be one of the big things that we are all very concerned about, as we should be. But just as you can have misuse, you can have appropriate use. Sometimes there is intentional misuse, and then sometimes there are good intentions that just end up with bad results, and we need to make sure we distinguish between them.

At the end of the day, however, patients have to understand all this and buy into it, buy into research. We know we only have three percent of cancer patients that accrue to clinical trials. That is already a low number. So, this is just making that worse. So, if we don't have uptake, then we don't have participation in research. If we don't have biospecimens—biospecimens are one of the largest rate limiting factors to drug discovery in this country right now. Biospecimens and privacy go hand in hand. No question about it.

At the NCI, there are important programs that are going on. Sarah spoke to a few of them. The National Biospecimen Network, the Prostate SPORE Pilot, but also The Cancer Genome Atlas Project. Now, that is a project that speaks exactly to privacy, we are going to have to deal with this very soon in a very big way because we are getting to the point of having to deal with it clinically and in real life. For a long time it has kind of been in theory. It has been what we are going to be able to do with research, and maybe we will be able to genetically predict something, but it is here now. So, without those biospecimens, we can't do the research. We don't have the progress. We don't have the answers. No cure or hope. That is not a good situation.

Are we achieving what we had hoped with the rules and the implementation of HIPAA? I don't think so. I think that everybody has had good intentions—the government, the researchers, everybody trying their hardest in spite of obstacles. I asked myself, or I ask you, what the benefit to the patient has been. So far I am not sure that I have heard much. I think that is kind of sad because I would have to say that there have been millions upon millions of dollars spent to do this. There is an entire industry now of people that go out and tell people how to comply with the regulations. So, had we spent all that money a little differently, spent it all on research, maybe we could have had a different outcome.

I am not saying "throw the baby out with the bathwater," but I am saying we need to look at risk and benefit from a financial investment standpoint again. But when they question some aspects of HIPAA and why they have to jump through all these hoops, patients also say, well, why are these people telling me what I have to worry about with my information. I respect very much the privacy rights people and the ethical people and everybody there because they do a good job, but I think it is a reasonable question: "why are people making the risk benefit decision as it relates to privacy, other than the patient?" While this may not be a good analogy, to a certain extent it is the same question as a woman's right to choose. I mean, it is a similar kind of thing if you think about it. Whose right is it? Who owns the biospecimen? Who should decide where the biospecimen goes? Who decides about my privacy?

We have talked a little bit about potential duplication in the regulation of research. Now let me briefly talk about the era of personal genetic information as it relates to what we are doing with the data, the sharing, the information, and the data release. I was just at a meeting a couple of weeks ago with The Genome Atlas Project, a bunch of great minds in the room. We spent a day and a half trying to figure out data release policies. So, I don't want to see you doing all this great science, and then we hit a wall and lose momentum because we don't have these issues addressed.

Also what the patient community is concerned about is that we see in the community and in the academic research centers that resources in the form of dollars and people are being redirected because they have to comply with regulations. So, we are shifting things around, and it is the scientists and patients who will lose in the end. That is a problem when we redirect these resources in a zero sum game.

So, Congress is going to have to cough up more money if they are going to keep putting these burdens and regulations on people, because you can't make unfunded mandates, and you have got to compensate appropriately people trying to do this work. Because that is like trying to do something with both hands tied behind your back and it really doesn't work at all.

I don't think I am sharing with this community anything that you don't already know. I would offer, however, based on my experience from eight years working on behalf of advocates, and also working very closely with the NCI, FDA, industry, and with researchers, that agencies and the research community (of which I consider industry a part) have really underutilized existing resources to assist in doing outreach and grass roots communication. Advocacy groups and qualified advocates are very valuable resources that they underutilize. These resources can be good partners to help communicate the message and connect the dots better across the agencies. Advocates sometimes have ways to help you create bridges that otherwise can't be created for whatever reason.

The demands of research necessitate that all of us figure out how to do that a little better, because people like myself, Paul, Mary Lou, others in the room, who represent the advocacy community are very willing to help. But we need to allow appropriate use of data and of specimens and all the research that goes with it to advance discovery. We need to make the research relevant to the people. We need to explain to them why it is relevant, because sometimes it is pretty abstract, and they can't understand: "What is in it for me," and "What does it mean to me and my family"—patient centered education and awareness—and we need to function at both the grass roots and the grass top level.

Why do we have to get it right? Well, I think it is really simple. I think we have to get it right because in the end, it is really all about the patient, and I do believe that the resources exist. I believe that there has been a lot of money invested, that there just needs to be a little stronger will, and when I say that, I think that it means that people need to put a little more skin in the game. They need to check a few more things at the door and not bring those to the table with respect to individual agency and organizational agendas. I think they need to go to a little higher level in putting some things aside that historically have been obstacles relative to siloization or just the way things were, encouraging greater transparency, encouraging greater collaboration.

I think NCI has done a marvelous job in trying to force that to a certain extent. For all of you who are the funding agencies or organizations in the room, I think that you can implement the golden rule. We all know the golden rule of the Bible, but I am talking about the golden rule of academic science, which is "he who has the gold rules" and can set the rules and can help bring people with the skills to hit the target that you are going to set.

I would say to the agencies go ahead and set the target. We will help you figure it out.

Ms. Smith: I was just asked to give some comments, which I would like to do now. First of all, I sit on Rush University Medical Center's IRB and have for seven years. So, I am intimately involved in this whole issue, and I know that it is not just that there is inconsistency among institutions' IRBs. We actually have more than one IRB, and we have differences among our own IRBs. So, we have some researchers that do IRB shopping trying to find the one they like best.

I attended a CaBIG Security Policy Project meeting recently. It was a great awakening to me to find out there isn't any way to de-identify information according to the technology experts in attendance. You can always find out who actually is attached to a piece of information. Given that and the fact that I would like to represent the patient view, I really am very interested in us doing a survey that looks at what the patient expects, not just the privacy of their financial information, but what they expect in relationship to research. What are their expectations of the risks and benefits of participating in research, and how do they want their privacy protected? I do think that we need to achieve the balance, and trust is very important. I also think transparency is important.

I believe that Paul Feldman's Health Privacy Project can be exceedingly helpful both in doing the survey because they have contacts with patients, and they are a trusted group. They can communicate to you what the patient issues are, and what the protections are back to the patient. The patients need to understand what their protections are and what HIPAA means to them.

I think we need to clarify what are best practices and ways of getting information about best practices out to the research community. Right now, there is not enough clarity and many varying interpretations of the HIPAA Privacy Rule.

Dr. Moses: Thank you, Paula and Mary Lou. Now we will turn to Carol Stocks.

Carol Stocks, Assistant Data Coordinator, AHRQ, Impact of the Privacy Rule on Health Services Research: I work at the Agency for HealthCare Research and Quality with a team of people that produce the HCUP databases, the healthcare cost and utilization project. Every year we collect hospital level administrative data with the help of many state level data organizations. Some of them are hospital associations, some are state agencies, and some of them are public health authorities. We collect a huge amount of this information; we now get about 90 percent of all of the hospital admissions in the United States, and from this information we create research databases. Health services research looks at the quality of health care, the cost of health care, and access to care. There are types of research that fall under the Common Rule, and there are types of health care research that involve large data repositories or survey information. So, you can tell from that description why we would be interested in the HIPAA Privacy Rule.

We decided to conduct a study about the impact of the Privacy Rule on health services research. We figured we were the ones most interested in this subject, and like everyone here today we had heard a lot of anecdotal information and concern about the effect of HIPAA on research. It was difficult for us to tell what was actually happening, what caused the fear, and in what way we might be able to help. So, through a contract with Abt Associates, with Dr. Deborah Walker as principal investigator and Daniel Friedman also an investigator, we set goals for the study of examining the initial effects that the Privacy Rule had had on health care research in the first 18 months after implementation of the Rule, and underlying that a goal to see if there was something that AHRQ could do to help.

Many of the questions in our study have already been discussed today. Are researchers avoiding certain types of studies based on changes in data release policy? Is restricted data access leading to bias in certain types of studies? That is very important to our agency. Are organizational policies being altered to reflect HIPAA compliance in ways that go beyond what the Privacy Rule intended? And there were many more questions. The literature review was started in July of 2004. We concluded the study, which I considered a phase 1, last summer. I will talk about that a little bit more in a minute. As you can imagine, there was not much literature out there that included quantitative data. There were six articles about the potential impact on researchers, and sixteen articles actually attempted to measure the impact on health services researchers. There were only four well-documented impact studies, six on impacts on registries and public health research, and six that reported some informal or indirect documentation.

We conducted interviews with 33 senior health care researchers, privacy officers, research compliance officers, and IRB directors. Since we were trying to explore what we felt would give us the best idea of what the impact was on health services research, we weren't necessarily focusing on clinical trials. We had 16 senior health services researchers and 17 privacy officers, research compliance officers and IRB directors involved. Our total response rate was 77 percent. Educational background was pretty high; 13 Ph.D.s, 7 M.D.s, 6 J.D.s, 6 master's degrees, 1 bachelor's degree. Our sample represented 18 states and all regions of the United States, a variety of health settings. We tried to cover the gamut, universities with medical and health components (8), some hybrid entities, medical schools (5), public health schools or departments (9), academic policy schools or centers (2), private health systems (5), research and consulting firms (3), and one state government representative. Thirty-one of the 33 responding settings had an IRB. Most universities we found had identified themselves as hybrid entities with the medical school and related services being covered entities, and all the research firms and schools of public health were non-covered entities.

In most cases, IRBs had the responsibility for both the Common Rule and the Privacy Rule, although some had a subcommittee to handle HIPAA matters. Privacy boards, at least at that time, were being utilized in only one of the settings. So, 94 percent reported that they perceived an impact from the Privacy Rule. Those reporting substantial impact were involved with multi-site studies where follow-up information from many patients was needed from many settings, as was noted several times today. They were experiencing a decline in patients agreeing to participate in research studies because of long and complicated consent and authorization forms, and they were experiencing a lack of participation from small hospitals and provider groups due to the lack of resources. This is disturbing because of the bias that we anticipate seeing in future research.

Not surprisingly, 90 percent reported increased costs and resources being expended. Eighty-seven percent reported increased times for IRB preparation and participant recruitment; 74 percent reported that they were concerned about bias. Problems obtaining consent of participants were reported from 68 percent, and conflicting IRB interpretations from 65 percent. I think it would be interesting to see what the rate of conflicting IRB interpretations was before the HIPAA Privacy Rule compared to what we consider conflicting now. I am not sure how to get at that but I think it would be interesting to see.

Sixty-five percent reported difficulty in working with multiple IRBs. That is not surprising from what we have heard. Forty-two percent reported that they had encountered institutions and providers that refused to participate in research because of problems related to HIPAA. Problems obtaining de-identified data were reported by 39 percent, as I recollect due to cost. Other problems involved obtaining waivers or expedited reviews through IRBs, as reported by 26 percent. Ninety percent of our respondents said that they had made changes in how they planned for and conducted research. This involved more budgeting for longer time periods to recruit, more budgeting for resources to obtain de-identified data sets. Almost half (45 percent) described a study that had been stopped or altered because of the HIPAA Privacy Rule. I think that we should be concerned about these numbers, because over the long term we are less likely to get information from vulnerable populations, rural, smaller community hospitals, and all of the small clinics out there. Those are the areas that are just going to be too difficult to deal with. They have no legal counsel. There is nobody to say it is okay to participate in the study, your patient's data will be safe. So, they are just saying no. They don't have the resources, and they are too uneasy about involving their patients.

So, 31 of the informants had experienced the impact of the Rule on health care research and suggested the following reasons. This, they said, is why I think it is happening. Fifty five percent said it was because of the way the Privacy Rule was written, and many of them referred to the complexity and certain areas that were difficult to understand. It just wasn't clear to them. Misinterpretations of the Privacy Rule, 61 percent felt that was an important reason for problems, and 61 percent blamed overly conservative interpretations of the Rule. And the problems were ascribed to all of the three reasons by 26 percent.

Our conclusions were, therefore, that the Privacy Rule has had a major impact on health services research during the first 18 months and that there are two types of impacts. Some could be ameliorated with increased time, resources, and clearer guidances; others would require considering changes in the Privacy Rule itself. We feel that we need to monitor the Privacy Rule. That has come up several times—that we need numbers. We need to know what is going on. I would love to do another phase of this study, and I think that we really need to do one, but this does not come at the top of budget priorities like patient safety, access to health care, and cures for disease.

Based on the responses we got, guidance is needed to address key issues of concern—consent and authorization forms that were a problem two years ago and remain so; accessing information using verbal consents that many people brought up as really needing to be used in informed consent in certain populations, in the international context, for example. People want more guidance in the area of preparatory work for research and, of course, the annoying de-certified data sets by statisticians.

We did begin to work on some materials as a result of this study. We have a template for a user friendly low literacy combined consent and authorization form. It is going through channels. There are two people who have taken that off of my plate, and they are trying to make it available as soon as possible. I don't know if anyone in this room has done something like that. I would like to hear if you have. Maybe we could combine our efforts. We did a small amount of testing in the cognitive laboratory setting to try and look at this language so that people could understand it. That is a problem. Testing was pretty shocking. Then we worked a little bit on some vignettes that demonstrated where oral consent can be used instead of a written consent. But that is really initial work.

Dr. Moses: Thank you. Now let us turn to Mark Barnes.

Mark Barnes, Esq., Partner, Ropes and Gray, New York, SACHRP Recommendations for Changes in the Privacy Rule Regarding Health Research: I think the reason that I was asked to talk today was to tell you about the Secretary's Advisory Committee on Human Research Protections' (SACHRP) review and recommendations of a couple of years ago when I was a member of that body. I had been a member of the National Human Research Protections Advisory Committee (NHRPAC) which was Secretary Donna Shalala's advisory committee that was subsequently transformed into SACHRP under Secretaries Tommy Thompson and Leavitt. It was while I was serving on those two committees that I was asked to prepare a letter for SACHRP to send to the Secretary of HHS and to the Advisory Committee to HHS about the problems that we had seen in the Privacy Rule.

SACHRP is a body that is appointed by the Secretary of Health and Human Services, maybe 11 or 12 people, and they are drawn not only from the academic medicine side but also from the humanities and social science side of research. So, the effect of HIPAA was on our minds primarily in the biomedical context, but we also considered the humanities and social science context. The complications of HIPAA in social science tend to be overlooked, but are important, especially in research universities. They don't have medical schools, but they do have graduate departments and programs in, for example, psychology, sociology, anthropology, social work, and education.

So, we prepared a letter dated September 1, 2004 after many presentations and much debate within SACHRP. Sue McAndrew came and presented to SACHRP. Joanne Pollak from Hopkins came and presented to SACHRP. Today is in some ways a reunion of a meeting that happened two or three years ago.

But let me go to what we did and what we recommended. There are a lot of people who just wanted human subjects research to be exempted from the HIPAA Privacy Rule. That was one of the positions expressed early on, for example, by the AAMC, but it just wasn't going to happen politically. Therefore, we focused our efforts and attention within SACHRP less on trying to undo the regulations than trying to work within the regulations, with slight amendments to the regulations or differences in interpretation or guidance in order to ease the plight of researchers who were trying to conduct research, while at the same time preserving to the extent possible the privacy interests of their subjects. There are about seven or eight specific recommendations that we made to HHS and each of them addresses a particular problem that we found in the application of the Privacy Rule regulations to human subjects research, both biomedical and social science.

Accounting was the first problem addressed in our recommendations. Those of you who know HIPAA know the requirement that deals with disclosure of identifiable health information for research purposes that is not permitted by an authorization. In these circumstances, a covered entity, primarily an academic medical center, a physician group practice, or a mental health facility, among others, is required to document in the individuals' medical records that were reviewed, who accessed the records, on what date, for what purpose, and how much of each record was accessed. So, in other words, retrospective medical chart review, if it involves disclosure to someone outside the facility, would require that every single reviewed record have that notation in it, an accounting of disclosures. There is a difference within HIPAA between uses and disclosures. Disclosures are essentially transmissions of the information outside of the single covered entity to a different covered entity or a non-covered entity. When your own employed medical staff, for example, looks at records then, because those people are within the covered entity, it is not a disclosure, it is a use. But for people outside of the covered entity, for example, from another medical center or an affiliated medical center, perhaps, then that would be a disclosure outside of the entity that would require an accounting. This has required that there be an enormous number of accountings done of all of these kinds of research disclosures that previously, frankly, went on for years without any patient ever complaining that their privacy had been violated and to our knowledge, at least, any particular problems emerging in retrospective medical records research.

Now, in response to some of the early criticisms—these rules went out, as you probably know, in waves, and there were some amendments to them—there was a particular amendment. When 50 or more records are disclosed, not pursuant to a research authorization signed by the subject, but instead, pursuant, for example, to a waiver of informed consent and a waiver of authorization granted by an IRB or privacy board, this amendment allowed the covered entity, instead of accounting in every record, to make a list of all of the studies that would have accessed the whole set of records during a time period. Then if a patient asked for an accounting of the disclosures, a list of all of the potential studies that had accessed a patient's records would be handed over instead of an individual accounting of what specific people had accessed the patient's records. It was meant to ease the process, but it means that, if an institution pursued it, patients are handed a list that could be a hundred pages of medical records reviews. It may scare patients to death and, in many cases, their records actually were not reviewed for all of those studies.

Then, if you use that exception, you are required as an institution, if the patients ask, to ease and assist their access to the researchers to see if their records really were accessed for that particular study. So, basically you have a choice under the way these rules are written. You can either record every single accounting in every single record when it is accessed not pursuant to an authorization, or you can use the exception for those record reviews that are 50 or more records. But whatever happens, it has resulted in a massive amount of attention, time, effort, and energy devoted to recording these disclosures in all of these medical records all over the country, and it can provide a disincentive for institutions to allow research studies involving over 50 subjects.

So, SACHRP said, after noting these problems, that we thought it ought to be sufficient, even for disclosures outside the covered entity pursuant to a waiver that had been granted by an IRB or privacy board, to inform patients when they come into the facility and they get their notice of privacy practices, that this is a research institution, or we assist research, and this is what happens here. This is not unrestricted access. This is access the way it was since the inception of the Common Rule. If you come here, that is what happens, and your coming here is implied consent to this kind of records research.

The second recommendation involved de-identification of data. I think all of you know that HIPAA has essentially a higher standard for de-identification of data than under the Common Rule's anonymization standard. You can anonymize data under the Common Rule, which, in most cases has never been interpreted as strictly by any IRB, research administrator, or institutional official as the de-identification standard set out by HIPAA. There is the discontinuity that even when something qualifies as anonymized under the Common Rule, it may not qualify as de-identified under HIPAA. We suggested that there be some kind of synchronization of the standards between research under the Common Rule on the one hand and HIPAA's Privacy Rule on the other, so that the strict de-identification standards be looked at to see if it would be possible to reduce the number of data elements that would have to be omitted, particularly in regard to things like address, zip codes, geographic subdivisions, treatment dates, et cetera.

The limited data set was designed as a particular exception within the HIPAA standards, that allows a covered entity to retain treatment dates, other dates of service, as well as geographic identifiers in a disclosure, just not specific street addresses, but there has to be a limited data use agreement between all the parties that are sharing the information. The result is that there are data use agreements all over the place; there are data use agreements that are just signed as a matter of course. At some point, the cost of compliance outweighs the benefit to the patient. Our thinking was that when it comes especially to the treatment date and the location, given that there have not been abuses that we know of in the past, given that IRBs and privacy boards can look at these issues and decide them, there should be a relaxation of the de-identification standard so that it would be synonymous with IRB or privacy board application of the Common Rule standard.

Review preparatory to research is another category that is an exception under HIPAA. Remember the HIPAA general rule is you can't disclose information without an authorization, except for treatment, payment, and operations. One of the exceptions is that you can go to a privacy board or an IRB sitting as a privacy board and get a waiver based on the minimal risk to privacy criteria. There is another exception, the so-called review preparatory to research exception. Here, individual researchers can look at records within covered entities to see if it is possible, for example, to test a hypothesis within that patient population, to try to understand the frequency of the disease or condition within the patient population, to look at patterns of treatment within a patient population, to try to design a study or write a protocol. Before the researcher accesses the records, he or she must sign a review preparatory to research agreement that pledges limitation of use to these purposes, that the researcher will not disclose the information outside the covered entity, and that the access is needed for the review preparatory to research.

Through a series of HHS interpretations, individual researchers have been allowed to use the review preparatory to research as a method of identifying prospective subjects and getting their contact information, and, if the researcher is within the covered entity, that researcher is allowed under HIPAA—maybe not under the Common Rule, but under HIPAA—to contact those patients to see if they want to come into the study. However, if you are a researcher outside of the covered entity, then you can identify people during review preparatory to research if the covered entity allows you to come in, but you can't contact people to ask them if they want to be in the study. That is because if you contact them, then you have exceeded the institutional bounds in lay person's language, whereas a researcher employed by the facility is already within the institutional bounds.

There are many documents that try to define and refine this distinction, but the basic problem is that for the voluntary medical staff at a large academic medical center—perhaps not Mayo or Sloan Kettering where people are directly employed, but a community hospital situation or an NYU type model, where some of the faculty are employed, but most of the faculty are community physicians who simply have privileges there—these researchers are for HIPAA purposes deemed to be outside the facility.

It seemed to us odd to have this striking discontinuity between the treatment of internal researchers, the employed physician at NYU, and the treatment of the external researcher, who is on the medical staff at NYU, but not employed and not part of the covered entity, but instead part of the faculty and the faculty practice plan. So, in the end we said rather than focusing on these fine distinctions between the internal and external researchers created by the preparatory to research interpretations, there should be a more functional definition. The key to the distinction and the ability of researchers to use protected health information should be based on whether the covered entity exercises effective control over that individual's activities. We would regard membership and privileges of medical staff, the ability to terminate medical staff membership, or discipline medical staff as being effective control, thus, bringing the external NYU medical staff member into the covered entity for purposes of this facet of the Privacy Rule. As I said, we weren't trying to undo the rules, just trying to fix them as best we could.

With regard to future uses of information and authorization for future uses, unfortunately HIPAA came along at a very uncertain time historically. This was at the time that all of us were beginning to understand the immense value of biorepositories and data repositories. We had always known they were valuable, and OHRP, researchers, IRBs, research administrators, and ethicists were beginning to grapple with what it means to have a biorepository and to what extent do you have to refer back to the terms of the original consent, either a treatment consent or a research consent, to know how the biorepository can be used. In addition, there are many different variables. Identifiers can be omitted, and the repository information can be anonymized under the Common Rule, but then if the consent didn't originally say that the data or the specimen or both would be anonymized, what does it all mean? Where are the lines? What should the rules be? Are the existing biorepositories or data repositories contaminated by their source and the way that they were gathered in the first place?

Leaving aside the research repositories, we also have huge pathology repositories created as the standard of care for storage of pathology specimens. These tissues and biopsies and the specimen slides are collected and stored under treatment consents. What does all this mean for future use? At the time that all of this was being considered, HIPAA comes along. It was a period of gestation in the national research community, but the HIPAA rules were essentially laid on top of all of this raging debate about the ethics and the laws around informed consent for biorepositories and data banks.

It was when NHRPAC, the Donna Shalala committee, originally commented on the application of HIPAA to biorepositories. We asked for a clarification, because I personally had represented places like Sloan Kettering and other cancer centers and hospitals and knew that they had these massive biorepositories, these specimen banks. I was thinking, if we just keep the specimen bank, is that itself a research activity that would require a waiver from a privacy board, even though there wasn't an actual IRB protocol for the storage activity itself? This is just storage before anything is used for a particular purpose. So, I said, naively, HHS can't mean that the storage activity itself (even though the specimens have not been used for research, and we don't know when and where or even if they will be used for research) is a research use, and therefore, it has to have a waiver or research authorization? You can't mean that, HHS, can you?

The answer came back in the original commentary, when HHS looked at the rules: of course, we mean that, HHS said. By the way if you have got these biorepositories and data banks and you are keeping them as a platform for future research and that is why you set them aside, you need an IRB protocol for that. It resulted in an interpretation not only of HIPAA but also in a new interpretation, or one that was not clear to us before, of the Common Rule. So these authorization requirements have now been layered on top of all of the other problems in the area of future research.

We have two particular problems with the authorization requirement. I think this was alluded to in what Sarah said in regard to some of the NCI issues. One problem is that an authorization is supposed to be for a very specific purpose. OHRP and even FDA have allowed consent to have broad purposes, specific purposes if you know them, but also broad purposes for future use, leaving the definition of the requirements for an authorization under HIPAA more restrictive in the breadth of purpose that is allowable. Therefore, when we consent people to future uses and disclosures under HIPAA, there is somewhat of an ambiguous area in regard to how broadly we can seek and get their authorization.

Because drafters did not want there to be confusion in the patients' minds about what they were signing, HIPAA requires that an authorization always has to be for a particular purpose and can only be for a particular research study, and it can't be combined with anything else. You can combine the informed consent for a study with the HIPAA authorization into one document, as long as it meets the requirement for authorization. That is the reason I took you through the interpretation that led to all this. What it means is that when you have a primary interventional study, and you want to set aside specimens, or data for potential specimens, or data themselves for potential future uses, you have got to have the primary protocol approved, but now to be compliant with HIPAA, you must also have a protocol approved to store the specimens. That means you need two authorizations. OHRP lets you combine the consents. NCI, as all of you know, has that little check mark—the patient can elect whether the specimen is saved for research or not; if saved, whether it can be used for cancer or other research purposes. But on the authorization side, there must be two separate authorizations.

We recommended that the Privacy Rule should allow authorizations in these situations to be combined, and we also said that there should be an attempt to allow broader drafting in the HIPAA authorizations in regard to the preservation, the maintenance, the updating, and ultimately the future research uses of these identified specimens or data themselves.

Now, this next is a somewhat obscure point, so I will spend little time on it, although it actually makes a great deal of difference for IRBs and privacy boards. Under the Common Rule there is a set of activities that would be human subjects research except for an exemption. You can look at identified records and record the data somewhere else in an anonymized fashion without a link, and OHRP does not look at that as a research activity under the Common Rule. It is an exempt activity because there is nothing being recorded that is identifiable and traceable back to the subject.

Under HIPAA on the other hand, that same activity in the context of a research study is itself a use of data that is not exempt from the requirements of HIPAA authorization or of a waiver from a privacy board or IRB. So, the bottom line is that there is an activity that is exempt under the Common Rule, but, because it involves identified data, it is not exempt under HIPAA. We basically said, please fix that discontinuity between the two Rules.

The next problem issue is international research. There is a little bit of commentary within HIPAA and the original Q&A. My example is that a covered U.S. research entity has a study going on in Zimbabwe, and its doctors, who are part of the U.S. covered entity, go over to Zimbabwe, and they look over the individually identifiable data of subjects in Zimbabwe. They look at the data; they use the data; they disclose the data and bring it back to the U.S. covered entity and give it to others in the research institution, and maybe subcontractors, like the University of Zimbabwe and the infectious disease department of the University of Zimbabwe. If they do that, then does HIPAA follow extraterritorially that researcher who is part of a covered entity?

As a lawyer, I think the answer to that is yes. In fact, I don't see how you can say it is not the case. There is a whole body of law on extraterritorial applications of law. These are generally laws that have important public policy purposes, criminal laws and the like. They tend to follow, and there is no exemption within HIPAA for the international activities of U.S. covered entities. So, this has resulted in some very odd situations, For example, there will be a study by a U.S. covered entity, but it is the public health school, which may not be covered, and it involves another covered entity and a medical staff member with an appointment there and part employment at another covered entity. A social work department in yet another academic institution is involved, and people from various parts of this constellation of U.S. institutions are going to the University of Zimbabwe and getting all these records and bringing the information back and sharing it. IRBs in all these institutions have access to the identifiable data in case there is a research integrity question.

So, to make a long story short, the international research implications of HIPAA are basically a mess and maybe they are meant to mean what I just said, but if so, we would like to have some guidance on it. We would like to be told how you do it, what you do and what it all means.

Ms. Pollak: There is an additional problem. Most of these countries have their own IRBs and their own consent forms. They will not agree to the dual consent form combining HIPAA authorization with informed consent. So, you end up with two forms, even if they are shortened. It is alarming to people; they think they are giving up some kinds of rights. Therefore, your participant pool goes way down. Based on our experience with this sort of thing, our IRBs believe that in certain countries it is impracticable to get informed consent or an authorization, and so they are waived. In those countries, researchers are just supposed to talk consent through with the subjects according to a script. But clarification would be helpful.

Mr. Barnes: Thank you because I was skipping over one of the recommendations in that regard a little too quickly. We requested that for international projects OCR allow us an alteration mechanism, through a privacy board or an IRB sitting as a privacy board, to condense that complicated HIPAA authorization to one or two paragraphs that are understandable in the cultural context of (in our example) Zimbabwe and our HIV prevention study there. Clearly, the form will not have everything in it. For example, it will not say as required by HIPAA (because nobody in Harare would understand it) that if pursuant to HIPAA we give your information to somebody not covered by HIPAA, and they disclose it, they will do so with impunity under U.S. law. I have never figured out a way to say that particular thing easily, but I guarantee there is nobody in Zimbabwe that will understand that. In fact, we have used a condensed authorization form in some cases, processing it through the IRB or privacy board for approval.

Finally, let me touch on access to protected health information by public health authorities which is a particular issue in cancer. HIPAA does not infringe on that access, but then there are agencies like AHRQ. The last I heard, HHS general counsel's interpretation was that AHRQ was not a public health authority. So, AHRQ would have to go through the HIPAA waiver process or obtain an authorization in order to get access to data.

There are public health authorities that do public health surveillance, but they also do public health research, and the line between what is public health research and what is the exercise of police power under public health has been a matter of some contention within the public health community. Every good health department has its own IRB and debates and decides these issues. However, for AHRQ, for other sorts of government quality assurance and research, for quality assurance agencies within the states, for other kinds of entities that follow-up people long term in databases in NCI and cooperative groups, there has been a great deal of confusion. Although I have not been involved intimately as I once was, since these issues have started to be resolved in the last couple of years, the last I left it, there were different parts of the NIH that had different views on how HIPAA applied to them. So, anyway, we asked that OCR determine that quality assurance agencies that are part of government, or quasi-government agencies, or agencies like AHRQ, are public health authorities so that they need not go through individual privacy board waivers or authorizations to do their work.

Those were our recommendations that we sent to Secretary Thompson. You have the recommendations and the background text that supports each of the recommendations in your briefing materials. To my knowledge, none of our recommendations has been adopted yet. So, I commend them to your attention.

Ms. McAndrew: I can report, on behalf of the department, that they were properly acknowledged, and they are under consideration.

Ms. Stocks: The matter of AHRQ being recognized as a public health authority has been addressed. There is a question and answer up on the OCR web site, and we have access as long as we use the data for public health purposes.

Dr. Moses: Any other comments or questions? We have come to the end of our discussion on HIPAA, which has been very informative for me, and I think some very interesting things have come out. I would like to thank all the invited speakers for their presentations and the members of the Forum and others for their comments and contributions to the discussion. There are no formal actions that the Forum can take to go further with this; that will be up to the IOM and others. But we could approve staff assistance to IOM helping to take this toward a committee study. So, the question is whether we can support that. If there is further work, this would be under an IOM Board. It would not be cancer specific, since I think we all agree this is a broad health and biomedical research issue; so, it is appropriate I think that it go to the broader IOM.

Dr. Burish: I am not against it, but are there other options? It has been a great session, and I just worry that there will be more meetings about more meetings. What are our options?

Dr. Moses: Let me respond. I think the best outcome that we could hope for would be a committee report with firm recommendations, and I'm told that IOM is interested in that option, and that NIH may be as well.

Ms. Carr: I certainly think that NIH is interested in facilitating further analysis of the issues, and we would want to see any study done very carefully so that it would get beyond some of the problems with the data that have been gathered so far.

Dr. Burish: I think you addressed my concern. I wasn't sure whether this group had the authority or authorization to take directly some of the actions you have talked about. Apparently, it does not. I am in favor of an IOM committee.

Ms. Boswell: As IOM designs a study, may I encourage you to not just focus on the economic impact of the Privacy Rule on the people that you survey. I think it is very telling that of the speakers that you felt you should invite to have a discussion today, most of them that were non-government people were lawyers. It's a bad sign if three years after implementation researchers need their lawyers in order to understand what they are supposed to be doing. Ask some questions to get at the involvement of others, even some that previously may not have been involved in research issues. I have never gone to a meeting about IRBs and the Common Rule where there were so many lawyers, but conversations about HIPAA always involve a lot of lawyers. I think that is a problem for our research. I think our research ought to be a lot more user friendly to the patients than to have lawyers being the folks that are so involved.

Dr. Ferrell: I want to state a compelling issue: almost everything we have heard today has been from the perspective of the researchers, the organizations, and institutions. I think it is really critical to hear the voice of the patients.

Dr. Moses: We have had two patient advocates.

Dr. Ferrell: I think we have glossed over Mary Lou's and Paula's comments that their groups, Y- Me, for example, are sources of information, and I am sorry that our Forum member, Ellen Stovall of the National Coalition for Cancer Survivorship, could not be here today. I hope IOM would seek out patient advocacy groups. I think we do need to hear what the patients with cancer who are participating in research want, and whether they understood what they signed, and how it could be done better for the patient.

Mr. Kean: Just one quick point, just for reassurance purposes. I am very supportive of doing this, but when you made the comment that this issue is much broader than cancer—and it is, and the IOM study should be broader than cancer—there were a lot of suggestions made today about focusing in just as you just did, Betty, on some of the cancer specific issues and the cancer centers. I would hope in carrying this out that doesn't get buried, because there are some cancer specific things that should be looked at.

Dr. Moses: I totally agree. We have actually discussed that, and I expect that IOM will keep those things in mind. Now, I would like to thank you all for your attention. This completes the workshop on the effects of the HIPAA Privacy Rule on health research.

Glossary

Accounting for Disclosures: Information that describes a covered entity's disclosures of protected health information other than for treatment, payment, and health care operations; disclosures made with Authorization; and certain other limited disclosures.

Authorization: An individual's written permission to allow a covered entity to use or disclose specified protected health information for a particular purpose.

Business Associate: A person or entity who, on behalf of a covered entity, performs or assists in performance of a function or activity involving the use or disclosure of individually identifiable health information, such as data analysis, claims processing or administration, utilization review, and quality assurance reviews, or any other function or activity regulated by the HIPAAA Administrative Simplification Rules, including the Privacy Rule. Business associates are also persons or entities performing legal, actuarial, accounting consulting, data aggregation, management, admistrative, accreditation, of financial services to or for a covered entity where performing those services involves disclosure of individually identifiable health information by the covered entity or another business associate of the covered entity to that person or entity.

Covered Entity: A health plan, a health care clearinghouse, or a health care provider who transmits health information in electronic form in connection with a transaction for which HHS has adopted a standard.

Covered Functions: Those functions of a covered entity the performance of which makes the entity a health care provider, health plan, or health care clearinghouse under the HIPAA Administrative Simplification Rules.

Data Use Agreement: An agreement into which the covered entity enters with the intended recipient of a limited data set that establishes the ways in which the information in the limited data set may be used and how it will be protected.

Designated Record Set: A group of records maintained by or for a covered entity that is (1) the medical and billing records about individuals maintained by or for a covered health care provider; (2) the enrollment, payment, claims adjudication, and case or medical management record systems maintained by or for a health plan; or (3) used, in whole or in part, by or for the covered entity to make decisions about individuals. A record is any item, collection, or grouping of information that includes protected health information and is maintained, collected, used, or disseminated by or for a covered entity.

Disclosure: The release, transfer, access to, or divulging of information in any other manner outside the entity holding the information.

Food and Drug Administration (FDA) Protection of Human Subjects Regulations: Regulations intended to protect the rights, safety, and welfare of participants involved in studies subject to FDA jurisdiction (Title 21 CFR, Parts 50 and 56).

Health Care Clearinghouse: A public or private entity, including a billing service, repricing company, community health management information system or community health information system, and "value-added" networks and switches that either process or facilitate the processing of health information received from another entity in a nonstandard format or containing nonstandard data content into standard data elements or a standard transaction, or receive a standard transaction from another entity and process or facilitate the processing of health information into a nonstandard format or nonstandard data content for the receiving entity.

Health Care Provider: A provider of services (as defined in section 1861(u) of the Act, 42 U.S.C. 1395x(u)), a provider of medical or health services (as defined in section 1861(s) of the Act, 42 U.S.C. 1395x(s)), and any other person or organization who furnishes, bills, or is paid for health care in the normal course of business.

Health Information: Any information, whether oral or recorded in any form or medium, that 1) is created or received by a health care provider, health plan, public health authority, employer, life insurer, school or university, or health care clearinghouse; and 2) relates to the past, present, or future physical or mental health or condition of an individual; the provision of health care to an individual; or the past, present, or future payment for the provision of health care to an individual.

Health Insurance Portability and Accountability Act of 1996 (HIPAAA): This Act requires, among other things, under the Administrative Simplification subtitle, the adoption of standards, including standards for protecting the privacy of individually identifiable health information.

Health Plan: For the purposes of Title II of HIPAA, an individual or group plan that provides or pays the cost of medical care (as defined in section 2791(a)(2) of the PHS Act, 42 U.S.C. 300gg-91(a)(2)) and including entities and government programs listed in the Rule.

Health and Human Services (HHS) Protection of Human Subjects Regulations: Regulations intended to protect the rights and welfare of human subjects involved in research conducted or supported by HHS (Title 45 CFR, Part 46).

Hybrid Entity: A single legal entity that is a covered entity, performs business activities that include both covered and noncovered functions, and designates its health care components as provided in the Privacy Rule. If a covered entity is a hybrid entity, the Privacy Rule generally applies only to its designated health care components. However, non-health care components of a hybrid entity may be business associates of one or more of its health care components, depending on the nature of the relationship.

Individually Identifiable Health Information: Information that is a subset of health information including demographic information collected from an individual, and (1) is created or received by a health care provider, health plan, employer, or health care clearinghouse; and (2) relates to the past present, or future physical or mental health or condition of an individual; the provision of health care to an individual; or the past, present, or future payment for the provision of health care to an individual; and (a) that identifies the individual; or (b) with respect to which there is a reasonable basis to believe the information can by used to identify the individual.

Limited Data Set: Refers to protected health information that excludes 16 categories of direct identifiers and may be used or disclosed, for purposes of research, public health, or health care operations, without obtaining either an individual's Authorization or a waiver or an alteration of Authorization for its use and disclosure, with a data use agreement.

Minimum Necessary: The least information reasonably necessary to accomplish the intended purpose of the use, disclosure, or request. Unless an exception applies, this standard applies to a covered entity when using or disclosing protected health information or when requesting protected health information from another covered entity. A covered entity that is using or disclosing protected health information for research without Authorization must make reasonable efforts to limit protected health information to the minimum necessary. A covered entity may rely, if reasonable under the circumstances, on documentation of IRB or Privacy Board approval or other appropriate representations and documentation under section 164.512(i) as establishing that the request for protected health information for the research meets the minimum necessary requirements.

Privacy Board: A board that is established to review and approve requests for waivers or alterations of Authorization in connection with a use or disclosure of protected health information as an alternative to obtaining such waivers or alterations from an IRB. A Privacy Board consists of members with varying backgrounds and appropriate professional competencies as necessary to review the effect of the research protocol on an individual's privacy rights and related interests. The board must include at least one member who is not affiliated with the covered entity, is not affiliated with any entity conducting or sponsoring the research, and is not related to any person who is affiliated with any such entities. A Privacy Board cannot have any member participating in a review of any project in which the member has a conflict of interest.

Protected Health Information: Protected health information is individually identifiable health information transmitted by electronic media, maintained in electronic media, or transmitted or maintained in any other form or medium. Protected health information excludes education records covered by the Family Educational Rights and Privacy Act, as amended, 20 U.S.C. 1232g, records described at 20 U.S.C. 1232g(a)(4)(B)(iv), and employment records held by a covered entity in its role as employer.

Research: A systematic investigation, including research development, testing, and evaluation, designed to develop or contribute to generalizable knowledge. This includes the development of research repositories and databases for research.

Transaction: The transmission of information between two parties to carry out financial or administrative activities related to health care. It includes the following types of information transmissions:

- Health care claims or equivalent encounter information
- Health care payment and remittance advice
- Coordination of benefits
- Health care claim status
- Enrollment and disenrollment in a health plan
- Eligibility for a health plan
- Health-plan premium payments
- Referral certification and authorization

The HHS Secretary is also required to adopt standards for first report of injury, claims attachment, and other transactions that the HHS Secretary may prescribe by regulation.

Use: With respect to individually identifiable health information, the sharing, employment, application, utilization, examination, or analysis of such information within the entity or health care component (for hybrid entities) that maintains such information.

Waiver or Alteration of Authorization: The documentation that the covered entity obtains from a researcher or an IRB or a Privacy Board that states that the IRB or Privacy Board has waived or altered the Privacy Rule's requirement that an individual must authorize a covered entity to use or disclose the individual's protected health information for research purposes.

Workforce: Employees, volunteers, trainees, and other persons whose conduct, in the performance of work for a covered entity, is under the direct control of the covered entity, whether or not they are paid by the covered entity.

SOURCE: Adapted slightly modified from the Glossary in *Protecting Personal Health Information in Research: Understanding the HIPAA Privacy Rule*. Posted April 14, 2003 and revised July 13, 2004. Accessed July 11, 2006 at http://privacyruleandresearch.nih.gov/pr_02.asp. Also, includes a personal communication to Roger Herdman from Christina Heide, OCR, DHHS, August 3, 2006.

Appendix

Workshop Agenda

Institute of Medicine
National Cancer Policy Forum
The Keck Center of the National Academies
500 5th Street, NW
Keck 201
Washington, D.C. 20001
June 16, 2006

8:15 am   Welcome, Opening Remarks
Harold Moses

8:30 am   HIPAA Privacy Rule and Health Research Discussion
Information on the Privacy Rule and Health Research from
the DHHS Office for Civil Rights
*Susan McAndrew, Acting Deputy Director for Health
Information Privacy, OCR*

9:00 am   Writing the Privacy Rule in DHHS
*Marcy Wilder, Partner, Hogan and Hartson, DC, Former
Deputy General Counsel and leader of the legal team advising on
the Privacy Rule, DHHS*

Raising Public Awareness of the Importance of Health Privacy
Paul Feldman, Deputy Director and Manager, DC Office, Health Privacy Project

9:55 am   Epidemiological Research and the Privacy Rule
Roberta Ness, Chair, Epidemiology, University of Pittsburgh Graduate School of Public Health, Director of Cancer Epidemiology, Pittsburgh Cancer Institute, Chair, Policy Committee, American College of Epidemiology

10:20 am   Break

10:30 am   Academic Health Center Research Impacts of the Privacy Rule
Joanne Pollak, General Counsel and Vice President, Johns Hopkins Health System

Privacy Rule Impact on Pharmaceutical Company Research
Donna Boswell, Partner, Hogan and Hartson, DC, PhRMA Representative for the Privacy Rule

Effect of the Privacy Rule on CDC and NCHS Research, Surveillance, and Public Health Programs
Ralph Coates, Associate Director for Science, Division of Cancer Prevention and Control, CDC
Catharine Burt, Chief Ambulatory Care Statistics Branch, Division of Health Care Statistics, NCHS

Negative Impact of HIPAA on Population-Based Cancer Registry Research
Dennis Deapen, Director Los Angeles Cancer Surveillance Program and Professor of Medicine, USC
(read into the record)

12:15 pm   Working Lunch

NIH Perspective: Questions about the Impact of the Privacy Rule on NIH Supported Research
Sarah Carr, Senior Advisor, Office of Science Policy, NIH

Patient Advocacy Perspectives: Importance of Balancing Privacy Protections and Research Data Sharing in Advancing Public Health
Paula Kim, President, Translating Research Across Communities Network

Other Advocate Comments
Mary Lou Smith, Y-Me Breast Cancer Organization and Co-Founder Research Advocacy Network

1:00 pm　Impact of the Privacy Rule on Health Services Research
Carol Stocks, Assistant Data Coordinator, AHRQ

SACHRP Recommendations for Changes in the Privacy Rule Regarding Health Research
Mark Barnes, Partner, Ropes and Gray, NY, Former Member Secretary's Advisory Committee on Human Research Protections

And Further Discussion

2:15 pm　Concluding Remarks and Adjourn Workshop